THE INDIE AUTHOR CHECKLIST

FROM CONCEPT TO LAUNCH AND BEYOND

ADAM CROFT

With more than 1.5 million books sold to date, Adam Croft is one of the most successful independently published authors in the world, and one of the biggest selling authors of the past few years.

His 2015 worldwide bestseller *Her Last Tomorrow* sold more than 200,000 copies across all platforms and became one of the bestselling books of the year, reaching the top 10 in the overall Amazon Kindle chart and peaking at number 12 in the combined paperback fiction and non-fiction chart.

His *Knight & Culverhouse* crime thriller series has sold more than 250,000 copies worldwide, with his *Kempston Hardwick* mystery books being adapted as audio plays starring some of the biggest names in British TV.

In 2016, the *Knight & Culverhouse Box Set* reached storewide number 1 in Canada, knocking J.K. Rowling's *Harry Potter and the Cursed Child* off the top spot only weeks after *Her Last Tomorrow* was also number 1 in Canada. The new edition of *Her Last Tomorrow* also reached storewide number 1 in Australia over Christmas 2016.

During the summer of 2016, two of Adam's books hit the *USA Today* bestseller list only weeks apart, making them two of the most-purchased books in the United States over the summer.

In February 2017, *Only The Truth* became a worldwide bestseller, reaching storewide number 1 at both Amazon US and Amazon UK, making it the bestselling book in the world at that moment in time. The same day, Amazon's overall Author Rankings placed Adam as the most widely read author in the world, with J.K. Rowling in second place.

In January 2018, Adam's bestselling book to date, *Tell Me I'm Wrong* became a worldwide bestseller and has since gone on to sell more than 250,000 copies.

Adam has been featured on BBC television, *BBC Radio 4*, *BBC Radio 5 Live*, the *BBC World Service*, *The Guardian*, *The Huffington Post*, *The Bookseller* and a number of other news and media outlets.

In March 2018, Adam was conferred as an Honorary Doctor of Arts, the highest academic qualification in the UK, by the University of Bedfordshire in recognition of his achievements.

Adam presents the regular crime fiction podcast *Partners in Crime* with fellow bestselling author Robert Daws.

facebook.com/adamcroftbooks

twitter.com/adamcroft

instagram.com/adamcroftbooks

INTRODUCTION

Independent publishing is a minefield. Whether you're working on your first book or you're a seasoned pro, there's an enormous number of things you need to remember to do.

Non-writer friends often ask me what I do all day. I presume they're coming from the same angle as I was before I wrote my first book: that my days are spent gazing out of windows and thinking up new plot ideas.

You're probably chuckling along with me right now. If you're not, panic. My humour only gets worse. But my point is that indie authors have to wear many hats.

We're writers, marketers, business owners, publicists, broadcasters, customer service executives and a hundred other things that would make this a long and boring paragraph if I carried on.

It's easy to forget something simple along the way to publishing a book. I have, at various times, forgotten to ensure books were edited in time for release day, missed pre-order deadlines and gone six months without adding my latest book to my website.

When my wife first started working with me just over two years ago, one of the first things we did was create a publishing checklist. That list has grown and changed over the past couple of years, but its purpose remains the same: to stop me mucking things up.

Two years later, in 2018, I released *The Indie Author Mindset* and launched its accompanying Facebook group (which is absolutely <u>awesome</u> and well worth joining if you're an indie author).

One of the first things I did was ask the group's members what they'd like me to write next. The most popular option was the concept for this book: a checklist for writing and publishing a book, from concept to launch and beyond.

If you're a new writer wondering what lays ahead, this book is the stark and honest truth laid out in a handy step-by-step guide to getting your book out there — and everything that happens afterwards. If you're one of those seasoned pros, perhaps it'll help you avoid a few silly mistakes of your own. Yes, you know the ones.

In any case, I hope you find it useful. If you want

to discuss any of the ideas covered in this book, or would like to hang out with a bunch of fantastically helpful indie authors, I strongly recommend checking out the official Indie Author Mindset Facebook group.

But not yet. You've got a book to read.

Let's get to it.

A NOTE ON STRUCTURE

It seems a little naughty of me to admit that a book designed to teach you a structured and organised approach to writing a book should, in itself, have had such an unstructured and disorganised birth. But it's true.

The fact of the matter is, no matter how structured and organised I try to be with my non-fiction writing, I end up having to abandon that neatness and revert to something a little more… Well, *me*.

There are a plethora of issues in this industry which need addressing. Those issues are tangents or even sub-tangents of the actual content and skeleton of this book, but they need addressing all the same.

There are also some handy tips, tactics and strategies which it'd be remiss of me to ignore or keep to myself. Although they might not strictly follow the 'checklist' structure, I've included them in order to give the book more colour and, of course, you more useful and practical advice to boost your book sales.

Each chapter has a summary at the end with all of the actionable and practical tasks laid out, and there's also an *actual* checklist at the end of the book which lays out my personal timetable and list of actions for planning, writing and launching a book.

It's worth me saying at this point that there's no definitively 'correct' way to do any of this. All I can say is that I've spent the best part of a decade doing some things right and most things wrong, and I've expended a lot of time and money testing what works. For me, this is it. For you, it might not be. It'll likely change for me in a couple of months, too. But this book — as with all advice I give — contains the underlying principles which, on the whole, do not change.

This industry is all about the long-term, and your approach to your writing career should match that.

So, please forgive me where I go off on a tangent. There are very good reasons for me doing so. And, once you've read the book from cover to cover, I'm confident you'll have a much improved grounding on the whole process from start to finish — a grounding which will enable you to write and sell more books from that moment on.

STAGE 1: PLOTTING AND PLANNING

GENRE

Yep, I'm getting onto one of the most contentious issues in publishing, right from the starting blocks. Don't worry — I tend to do this.

If you've at least dipped your toes in the indie pool (come on in, it's warm!) you'll know it's similar to the traditional publishing world in many ways, and different in many others.

I see the relationship between trad and indie as a Venn diagram, with a lot of overlap but some distinct and important differences. Genre is something which can be described as a similarity *and* a difference.

Genre is important. That's something the traditional publishing world has known for some time, and which is true. Giving readers an idea — at first glance — of what genre your book falls into is something which will make your marketing efforts much simpler in the long run.

But this is an area in which traditional publishers have it a little easier.

With wider marketing avenues — and larger budgets — traditional publishers can try to push genre expectations and sway readers towards trying something new. That's tricky online. Let me explain why.

Online, when it comes to books, readers tend not to browse as much. They certainly don't browse in the same way. They tend to look for things which are familiar whereas readers browsing a bookshop are often looking to be swayed or influenced.

Cross-genre books or novels which can't be pigeonholed will often stand out from the crowd with a clever marketing plan behind them. Think *Life of Pi*, for example. It's a great novel, without a doubt. But what the hell *is* it?

Indies don't have that luxury. Readers don't know us, and they're swimming in a pool of books — no, drowning in it. There are literally millions of books available online — far, far more than in even the biggest bookstore — so readers tend to gravitate towards safety, and what they know and love.

And that's why it's so important that you know what genre your book is in before you start writing it. If you want to write something different and fresh as a vanity project, that's great. But if your intention is commercial, it's always best to make sure the book fits within a predetermined genre — and one which preferably has readers.

But what if you've already written a book and it doesn't fit into any predetermined genre?

Cross-genre writing is popular. There's no doubting that. It's popular in the sense that a lot of people do it, but not in that many people have success with it. Some do, but it's difficult.

My advice would be to bear both genres in mind, try marketing towards both and see what works best. Whose books are yours similar to? Write a list of authors, and pigeonhole *those* authors into genres. Which genre has the most names in it?

If you're sitting there thinking '*My books aren't similar to anyone else's. I've written something truly unique*' then you're either wrong or you've just made a huge mistake.

All books are similar to other people's. There are only a finite number of actual stories (some people say as few as six) and books need to conform to a certain set of expectations. In the same way you can't just invent new musical notes, you have to stick to the expected forms of writing, too.

Readers have expectations. They want books they know they're going to like, because they've liked similar books in the past. If you've written something truly unique, which has never been seen before, you've just made selling the thing a thousand times harder.

THE HOOK

Hooks are something I've become known for. As is ending a sentence on a preposition.

My first really successful book was *Her Last Tomorrow*, which carried the following hook:

Could you murder your wife to save your daughter?

The book was an incredible success, mainly because its hook allowed me to market it in a fresh and innovative way.

That book wasn't a one-off. I repeated it with another psychological thriller, *Tell Me I'm Wrong*, for which the hook was:

What if you discovered your husband was a serial killer?

That book went on to out-sell *Her Last Tomorrow* within a couple of months (HLT had been out for two-and-a-half years at that point) and is now my all-time biggest seller.

In a moment, I'm going to tell you why those hooks worked. But first of all I need to make something abundantly clear.

Following my formula will not work for you.

Well, it probably won't. Let me explain.

My hooks work because they sing along with the backing music of the genre. They're psychological thrillers, also (and more relevantly in this case) called domestic suspense, domestic noir and domestic thrillers.

There are elements in both hooks which are congruent to the readers and their expectations within that genre:

1. DOMESTICITY

The hooks show that the book is clearly set within the domestic world.

*Could you murder **your wife** to save **your daughter**? / What if you discovered **your husband** was a serial killer?*

It implies a scenario in which our characters are ordinary people, to which something extraordinary happens.

2. THE TWIST

This is where the ordinary becomes extraordinary. This is where the domestic becomes noir.

Could you **murder your wife** *to save your daughter? / What if you discovered* **your husband was a serial killer***?*

It's the sort of bolt from the blue which turns the domestic situation on its head and makes readers think 'Woah, I gotta read that!'

3. PERSONALISATION

The hooks speak directly to the reader, rather than telling them about a character they don't know or care about.

Could **you** *murder* **your** *wife to save* **your** *daughter? / What if* **you** *discovered* **your** *husband was a serial killer?*

A word of caution. This doesn't work for all genres. It doesn't even work for my other thrillers or crime books.

Psychological thrillers are often written in the first-person, allowing the reader to put themselves in the shoes of the narrator or protagonist. This is something fans of the genre have come to expect, so wording the hook in this way makes it clear it's the sort of book they'd enjoy.

4. THE IMPOSSIBLE QUESTION

Both hooks ask the reader what they'd do. Not only that, but they're both an absolute mind-fork of a question to ask somebody.

Psychologically speaking, questions demand answers. People can't help but feel they've got to respond in some way. That response, that two-way relationship between the text and the reader forms a powerful bond which goes a long way towards convincing them to buy.

As you've probably noticed, it's going to be difficult for most writers of most genres to apply any of that to their own books. It's even difficult for me to apply it to *my* other books.

All I know is that it works for my psychological thrillers and the stories I write within that genre. And it's not just the genre and my name doing it, either. I've released other psychological thrillers between those two books which haven't been anywhere near as successful.

But these two have responded particularly well to marketing as I can hook readers in with just one short sentence. And that, right there, is the key. If you can find nine or ten words — at most — which utterly *compel* readers to buy your book, you're onto a winner.

That's something you can only do by knowing who your readers are, which genre you write in and what the readers' expectations are of that genre. Are they after action? Conflict? Romance? Aliens? All of those things?

Those are the questions you have to answer in order to generate a super-marketable hook which will work for *your* books in *your* genre.

Some of the principles can be translated to some other genres. For example, the personalisation aspect might work for romance but probably wouldn't for sci-fi. Why? Because romance readers are more likely to project themselves onto the book characters (and vice versa) than sci-fi readers are.

The key, as always, is knowing your readers and knowing *why* they read that particular type of book. Once you know that, you'll be able to come up with a hook that speaks to them.

BUILDING A SKELETON

After I've developed my hook or my 'what if' situation, the next step for me is to plan the overall skeleton of the book.

It might sound obvious, but you'd be amazed how many books I come across which don't have a beginning, a middle and an end.

Of course, *all* books have some form of beginning, middle and end — but not always in the story sense.

Your **beginning** needs to have some form of **inciting incident** which upsets the status quo and introduces the journey your main protagonist has to go on. This is the story we'll be following.

Harry Potter gets his letter from Hogwarts. Luke Skywalker accidentally hears Princess Leia's message. In *The Shining*, Jack accepts a job at the Overlook hotel.

Your **middle** needs to have some form of **irre-**

versible event halfway through the book which turns everything on its head and propels the story forward towards the end.

In *Jaws*, Police Chief Brody comes to realise he must change his strategy and attack the shark in its own habitat. Harry Potter saw Voldemort drink the unicorn's blood and had a new resolve not to let Voldemort obtain the Philosopher's Stone. Frodo Baggins says 'sod the lot of you' and decides to take the ring to Mordor himself.

It's a change in direction, and it needs to happen as close to the middle of the story as possible.

Look out for a major incident next time you're watching a movie. Now you know what it is, you'll spot it. Pause it and you'll see you're almost exactly halfway through. That's the midpoint twist.

Your **end** needs to provide a satisfying conclusion, give the reader some form of closure in an epilogue (although it needn't be named as one) and tie up all the story's loose ends.

Story structure is a huge subject, and one best tackled in another book, but a strong beginning, middle and end will set you on the right course.

Here are some examples of beginnings, middles and ends of previous books of mine:

HER LAST TOMORROW

Beginning: Nick's daughter is kidnapped and he receives a ransom note.
Middle: Nick realises his only way out is to kill Tasha.
End: The kidnapper is discovered, normality returns but with serious lessons learned.

ONLY THE TRUTH
Beginning: Dan discovers his wife's dead body in his hotel bathtub.
Middle: Dan finds his confidante and companion, Jess, murdered.
End: Showdown with the killer, normality returns but with serious lessons learned.

IN HER IMAGE
Beginning: Alice Jefferson meets a new friend, who begins to stalk her.
Middle: Having only the police to turn to, Alice discovers her stalker is actually a serving police officer.
End: Showdown with the stalker, normality returns but with serious lessons learned.

Those three books are all very different from each other, but all follow the same form and recipe. Don't be afraid of this — it's what readers want and expect.

The structure and form of story have been

ingrained in our brains since we lived in caves. Trying to deviate from that structure is akin to trying to invent new musical notes. It will feel discordant and wrong.

Once you've got your beginning, middle and end it's time for the next stage: putting some flesh on that skeleton.

PUT ON SOME FLESH!

My next step is to take that beginning, middle and end and expand it out into a full synopsis.

This usually takes up one or two sides of A4, and should simply be a reeling off of what happens in the book. *First this, then this, then this.*

Think of it as a short-form version of the book, or a version for kids. You've got to tell the whole story on a sheet or two of A4. So no dialogue, no detail — just a list of events.

Imagine you're telling a friend what happens in the book, from start to finish. That's the sort of thing you're aiming for.

Here's the synopsis I wrote for my biggest selling book, *Tell Me I'm Wrong*.

If you've already read the book, you might note some differences between this synopsis and the finished book. That's fine. At this stage, the synopsis is just a guideline.

I always liken the planning stage to programming your car's sat nav before setting off. You know where you need to end up, and your sat nav has planned the route. However, if there's traffic on the way it might well re-route itself to take you a better way. It's the same with story.

PLEASE NOTE: The following text (quite obviously) contains spoilers. Please skip to the next chapter if you intend to read *Tell Me I'm Wrong*. You can come back and read this later.

Megan Miller is a woman whose life is changing. For years she's courted routine. She's always lived in the same village, had the same job since she left school, the same boyfriend — now her husband — since she was *at* school and a life of predictable regimen that kept her happy. Now, though, she finds herself at home on maternity leave with a newborn baby and a mind and body that's changing by the day.

She's not coping well with their newborn daughter, Evie. Evie was never able to feed properly and has never slept through a full night. Megan has been drinking heavily, which has added to the problems. Her husband, Chris, is a teacher at the local village primary school. He'd usually be around during the school holidays to help out but their relationship is fracturing to the point where he's spending more time out fishing than he is at home. Money is extremely tight. Chris's parents have often been taking Evie during the day just to give Megan a chance to sleep and recuperate.

The local and national news has been dominated by the story of a young boy murdered in a local park. The boy and his family were well known in the village, which is a small and tight community. He went to Chris's school, and was in his class. Whenever it's mentioned, Chris clams up. He doesn't want to talk about the boy. While Chris is out one day, Megan finds a blood-stained cap in the wheelie-bin. She doesn't recognise it as belonging to Chris and besides, it's too small; more like something a child would wear.

She dismisses it as circumstantial. It's a coincidence. She's known Chris since she was a kid and he's never even said 'boo' to a goose. There must be another explanation. Her suspicions are allayed until she begins to find more evidence linking Chris to the murder. Gifts from the boy to Chris are found hidden in a shoebox at the back of a wardrobe. She doesn't know where he was that day and she's starting to wonder what she knows about him at all.

She decides to confront him. She offers him the possibility that it could have been an accident. Maybe he hadn't meant for the boy to die. They can work this out together. His response comes like a bolt from the blue: he slaps her round the face and pushes her up against the wall. He quickly comes back into himself and apologises profusely. He hasn't slept much either, he's stressed up to the eyeballs and the death of one of the kids in his class and community has tipped him over the edge. He's never been violent before. Can she forgive him?

Megan knows her mind is likely playing tricks on her. She knows she's really not in a good place. She goes to speak to her doctor, thinking she's probably got some form of post-natal depression. The doctor isn't so sure that's the case, but then Megan isn't telling her the full story. She hasn't mentioned thinking her husband is a murderer.

Shortly after this, a second young boy is found dead in the village. He's been strangled in a muddy field near a stream. Again, the child was a student at the local village primary school. The deaths are inextricably linked. Later that day, Megan finds blood stains in the bathroom sink and mud on the floor near the back door. Megan now knows the first boy's death can't have been accidental. If Chris killed him, he did it deliberately, and he's done it again.

Feeling helpless, her mind spins out of control.

They've both always wanted a boy. Chris has always spoken about wanting a son. They both believed they couldn't have children, and had been trying for years, and when they'd found out they were having a girl she remembers Chris looking crestfallen. Is this some sort of 'revenge' psychosis?

She realises this is mad, and goes back to the doctor. She explains her thoughts and expresses how unreasonable she knows it sounds. She doesn't mention the evidence she's found. The doctor prescribes her anti-psychotics.

The national media frenzy is now huge. Megan has a crisis of conscience and realises enough is enough. She confronts him again, and this time she's prepared. She's phoned the police. Chris tells her he's had enough. He can't cope with her being like this. He's leaving her. The police arrive and speak to them both. They take Chris in for questioning.

Chris is eventually released from custody. There's not enough evidence to do anything. Because Megan didn't act on the blood-stained cap, the bins have been collected and the cap can't be traced. The hidden gifts, blood and mud can all be explained away. Chris says he hid the gifts because he couldn't cope with the death of his student and didn't want the reminders. The blood, he says, was because he cut himself shaving. The mud on the floor was because he'd been out fishing.

Megan realises she's lost her marriage and her mind. Chris doesn't come home. Megan is left disconsolate. She runs through everything in her mind. The clues were all there. The evidence was insurmountable. It *had* to be Chris. There's no way it couldn't be. Apart from her, the only person it could have been was Chris. *Apart from her*.

She scrambles for memories as she tries to piece everything together. On the date of the first murder, Evie was with Chris's parents. She was having her recuperation time. In reality, that meant trying to catch up on sleep but mostly getting blind drunk, having endless sobbing fits and experiencing retrospective blackouts. The anti-psychotics are doing their job. She's thinking far more clearly and rationally now. And she wishes to God she wasn't. She has flashbacks in which she remembers what she did. Not only did she kill the two boys, but on the second occasion she left Evie in the house alone.

In her mind, she's seen Chris wanting a boy and getting a girl. Then she's seen him become distant from her and spend more time away from home after the birth of Evie. Her brain put that down to him resenting her. In her unbalanced mental state, she thought she was doing this for him. Whichever way this ends, her marriage is over. Her daughter will lose at least one parent — not that she ever really had them anyway — and three local families have been torn apart by what she's done.

Megan is faced with two options. She can hand herself in to the police, which would effectively ruin Evie's life before it has even really started, not to mention what it would do to Chris and the local community. He'd never teach again. He and Evie would be ostracised by the local community forever. Or she can end her own life, which will have a profound impact on Evie and Chris but will, at least, allow them to eventually move on and build a new life as well as sparing the community any more hurt. Sooner or later memories will become hazy and life will go on. With a recent history of post-natal depression and psychosis on her medical record, she leaves a suicide note for Chris explaining that she's doing this for the sake of him and Evie, heads down to the water's edge, takes a huge overdose of her medication and lies down in the stream.

In the epilogue, we see Chris and Evie beginning to rebuild their lives. The village community is beginning to move on and the people have become closer as a result of what's happened.

Once you've got something like this, it's time to get going with the beats.

DROP THE BEAT(S)

Beats are the punctuation marks of your novel. They're the dramatic events and moments that define how your story moves forward.

Essentially, they're a pared-down list of events from your synopsis.

If you write using Scrivener (and you really should) I'd highly recommend making each beat a separate chapter file.

For me, my beats become chapters. Each chapter has an event that moves the story forward. If it doesn't, it's not a beat and it certainly isn't a chapter.

In my Scrivener file, the chapter name is the title of the beat (the bold text in the list below). Scrivener has a handy 'Synopsis' box, in which I go into a little more detail about what happens in that chapter.

Let's have a look at an example, with my first few beats from *Her Last Tomorrow*:

The family breakfast

Getting the kid ready for school. General daily routine. Happy families.

The kidnapping

Wife has gone to work. Getting daughter ready. There's a knock at door. He ignores it. In the car, about to leave for the school run as they're late (again — has to drive her in more often than not). As they're about to set off he realises he's forgotten something (something she needs for school?) and runs back into the house for two seconds to grab it. Comes back out and she's gone.

Reaction and search. Calls police.

He runs around the streets looking for her but can't find her. Calls police. Calls his wife too. She heads home, but will take a while.

The police arrive

He expresses surprise. Says he thought police didn't normally get involved until after 24 hours had passed. Police think this is a bit suspicious, tell him if it's a small child and under circumstances such as this, they spring into action right away. He shows the police some newspaper cuttings as they made the papers when they had her, due to her being a 'miracle child'.

Suspicion falls on the neighbour

He starts to suspect his neighbour. Elderly man. Lots of local stories about him being a pervert. Busybody who sees everything that goes on but says he somehow didn't see this when asked.

Police come back with more questions

Wife is back home. Police arrive again. They say they've spoken to the neighbour as well. Not only did he not see anything going on, but he claims he didn't see the daughter being put in the car in the first place. Only person's word is our protagonist's. In fact, the neighbour knocked at the door a bit earlier because the postman delivered to the wrong address and it wasn't answered. Where was he?

A ransom note is received

He receives a ransom note. It tells him he can have his daughter back but he must first kill his wife.

Each one of those paragraphs (or beats) became a chapter. So I could easily see an overview of my book as I wrote, the bold titles were the chapter titles (I renamed them Chapter 1, 2, 3, etc just prior to publishing) and the expanded text sat in the Scrivener sidebar as a constant reference point for me.

When I sat down at my desk each day to write

Her Last Tomorrow, I had a list of chapters with brief titles and a synopsis of what was going to happen in that chapter. Then all I had to do was write the scene out in full.

There was no danger of me not knowing what to write next. From that point on, I became a one-man word production line.

Once you've laid out your beats, you're ready to begin writing your novel.

1. Decide on your book's genre. It has one.
2. Try to develop a marketable hook for your book. It'll make life much easier (and money-filled) in the long run.
3. Determine your beginning, middle and end.
4. Build this out into a full synopsis.
5. Extract your story's beats and note these down. These are now your chapters.

STAGE 2: THE INEVITABLE ROADBLOCKS

I'M STUCK. NOW WHAT?

I know, I know. I made it sound easy, didn't I?

Anyone who's ever written a book, no matter how well planned, will know it doesn't quite work like that. The best-laid plans of mice and men often go awry, as the old poem goes.

There are a number of roadblocks you can run into whilst writing your book. And that's fine.

One of the most common is that **your story takes a new direction**. That's not necessarily something you need to be scared of. Many of my books have done this, and have been all the better for it.

If that happens, go back to your skeleton — your beginning, middle and end. Does it still work with your new direction? Revisit your synopsis and beats, and amend them to suit the new direction of your story. Then you can sit back in the saddle and carry on writing.

Some writers struggle with **productivity** when they know what's coming next. It's why many people are scared to plot their books in advance. Personally, I don't get this. I find it *much* more exhilarating to know what's coming and to be in control of what's conveyed to the reader, as well as when and how.

If this is an issue for you, why not leave a few details out in your synopsis? You may run into other difficulties if things aren't planned assiduously, but the main thing is that you get the book written in the best way for you.

There are some ways to get things moving again, though. Let's take a look at some of my favourites.

VISUALISATION

It might seem as if I'm going off on a slight tangent here, but bear with me.

One of the most powerful psychological tools a person has in their arsenal is visualisation. It sounds bizarre to say it, but simply visualising an end goal can have extraordinary power.

Natan Sharansky was a computer specialist who spent nine years in solitary confinement in the USSR, having been accused of spying for the United States. He passed the long, lonely hours by playing games of mental chess. He even said at the time 'I might as well use the opportunity to become the world champion!' In 1996, Sharansky beat Garry Kasparov, who at that time was the world chess champion.

You can get more than just psychological power from visualisation, too. Exercise psychologist Guang Yue from the Cleveland Clinic Foundation in Ohio studied visualisation in two groups of people. He wanted to find out if simply imagining exercise would be enough to have a benefit. They looked at brain patterns in weightlifters, and at what happened in the brain when they lifted hundreds of pounds. Remarkably, they found that the same areas of brain began to fire when the weightlifters simply *imagined* lifting that weight.

Spurred on, Guang Yue compared one group of people — who would go to the gym and do real weightlifting — against a second, who would simply carry out virtual workouts in their heads. The gym-going group saw a 30% increase in their muscle mass. But what was even more remarkable was that the group who simply imagined doing the workouts in their heads saw increases in muscle mass of up to 13.5% — almost half that of the actual bodybuilders — without lifting a finger. What's more, the muscle mass increase remained for three months after they stopped visualising.

Wherever you turn, successful people put a lot of stock in visualisation. World champion golfer Jack Nicklaus famously said 'I never hit a shot, not even in practice, without having a very sharp in-focus picture of it in my head'.

As a struggling comic actor in 1987, Jim Carey visualised being hugely successful and wrote himself a cheque for $10 million for 'acting services rendered', dated 1995. By that date, he was earning more than $10 million per movie.

Visualisation — simply seeing the outcome you want to achieve — is a hugely powerful tool. I've used it myself. Ten years ago when I started out writing and publishing, I photoshopped a screenshot of my online banking and added a few zeroes. I added it to a folder with photos of my dream cars, a beautiful house and photoshopped images of my books at the top of the charts. I, like other people who've seen the power of visualisation, credit it for a lot of my success.

It might sound pie-in-the-sky and wishy-washy, but what have you got to lose? Keep a strong image in mind of where you're going and you'll be amazed by what happens.

Fortunately, there are some practical ways you can put visualisation into practice if your progress on your book is starting to slow. There are two things I often do at this stage in order to harness the power of visualisation. Let's take a look at them over the next two chapters.

COMMISSION A COVER

Covers are absolutely vital to the success of books. I always say 'Never judge a book by its cover, unless it's a book'.

Lots of authors assume this doesn't matter, and that they can either design their own cover or get it done cheaply. Trust me — I've done both, and it *doesn't* work. Whatever your sales figures with a self-designed or cheaply-designed cover, you can easily treble them with a professionally designed cover.

I've worked closely with Stuart Bache on a number of my cover designs, and I never cease to be amazed at the things he and other professional designers take into account.

They know what typography to use, what blend of colours and what elements are scientifically proven to work for your genre of book. Even if you're an experienced graphic designer (which I am), book covers are a whole different ballgame.

I tend to commission a cover at one of three stages: before I start writing the book, partway through writing it or once it's finished.

Which of the three I opt for depends entirely on how the book's going.

COMMISSIONING A COVER BEFORE I START WRITING

Sometimes I have the title for a book before I've even started writing it. It's rare, and even rarer nowadays, but it does happen.

It's always good to get things moving as early as possible, and having the cover ready means you can do a cover reveal to your readers and fans earlier than usual, allowing you to build up some extra pre-launch buzz.

I've even been known to share a book cover with my readers and put the book up for pre-order before it's even half written.

Seeing the cover in the flesh can bring the book to life and spur me on to write it, too.

COMMISSIONING A COVER PARTWAY THROUGH WRITING

If you've run into a roadblock and you're feeling jaded about your book, this can be a great way to reinvigorate you and help you get enthused about the book again.

Just seeing your name and title on a cover can spark something creatively and give you your writing mojo back.

This is usually the way I do things. Once the writing is underway, it's usually a couple of weeks before I reach the middle and feel myself slowing down. That's when I commission the cover and give myself the spark to get over the finish line.

COMMISSION A COVER ONCE THE BOOK IS FINISHED

Sometimes there's no other option. There have been many times when I've finished a book and still had no idea what to call it. There've been other occasions when the release date has been held back because of it. No title means no cover.

Of course, on occasion you need to have the whole book written before a theme becomes apparent — which is often what leads you towards your final title.

The fact is that you need to commission your

cover whenever works best for you. If you're open to recommendations, I'd suggest getting it done about halfway through your book. Themes are usually apparent by then, and it could give you the extra boost that helps you through that awkward fallow spot after the middle of the book.

WRITE THE BLURB

The blurb (or, to give it its proper name, product description) is something else that will often enthuse me and spur me on towards getting a book finished.

There's a psychological aspect to this, which is actually quite interesting.

When writing a blurb or book description, you will — if you're doing it properly — be writing sales copy rather than simply describing the book. You don't want to tell people what happens — you want to sell them the book and let them find out for themselves.

In doing this, you're psychologically selling the book to yourself, too. There's an old saying that the first rule of sales is to believe in the product you're selling. By writing that blurb or product description and making your book sound awesome, you're selling your book to yourself and further enthusing yourself about it. That can easily be enough to lift you out of a block or fallow period during the writing of your book.

Of course, there's nothing to say that you need to write the blurb at this stage of the process, but I've put it here as I personally find it helps me to 'see' the finished product in as many ways as possible.

Seeing the end product, and having that spur you on to finish, is the power of visualisation at its finest. With a physical representation of the finished book cover and blurb, all that's needed now is for you to get the writing done.

PRACTICAL TIPS

Blurbs and product descriptions are tricky things. We all think we know what they are. But the vast majority of us are completely wrong.

This is one of those 'do as I say, not as I do' moments. Most of my blurbs and product descriptions are pretty awful. I'm working on revamping them as we speak. With that in mind, let's have a look at one of my worst and pull it apart.

Here's the current blurb for *Exit Stage Left*, the first in my Kempston Hardwick Mysteries series:

Charlie Sparks brought a whole new meaning to dying on stage...

Charlie Sparks had it all. A former primetime television personality, his outdated style has seen him relegated to the scrapheap.

When he collapses and dies during a stand-up routine at a local pub, mysterious bystander Kempston Hardwick is compelled to investigate his suspicious death.

As Hardwick begins to unravel the mystery, he quickly comes to realise that Charlie Sparks's death throws up more peculiar questions than answers.

Pretty horrendous, right? If you're wondering why I think that, let me show you.

Firstly, the blurb does what so many blurbs do: it summarises the plot. This is a **bad** idea. Almost every blurb writing expert advises against this. And there are very good reasons.

Think about it. You want the reader to buy and read the book. So why tell them what happens before they've even bought it?

At this point you're looking to sell them the book, and every word that simply rehashes the plot is wasted screen real estate on which you could be convincing potential readers to buy.

There's nothing in my blurb for *Exit Stage Left* that does that.

Ideally, your blurb should consist of a short opening sentence which grabs the eye and makes the reader want to go on to the next line. The second line should then make the third irresistible. All of that should be followed up with a call to action or line which makes them feel compelled to buy.

In my *Exit Stage Left* blurb, there's nothing about 'Charlie Sparks brought a whole new meaning to dying on stage…' that draws readers in. It's a pretty poor joke, but it does set up the fact that this particular series has a humorous bent and doesn't take itself too seriously. Even so, I think there are better ways of doing that.

The first line simply tells us who Charlie Sparks is.

> Charlie Sparks had it all. A former primetime television personality, his outdated style has seen him relegated to the scrapheap.

Who cares? No-one knows who Charlie Sparks is, and they don't give a damn. This mistake is made by authors the world over, who start their blurbs along the lines of *Character X is a Y who's always wondered why…*

Yawn. We all know that readers don't care about that sort of backstory and exposition until they've connected with a character in our books, and that goes for blurbs too.

Nor is there anything in that first line which draws readers onto the second, which is just as dreadful.

When he collapses and dies during a stand-up routine at a local pub, mysterious bystander Kempston Hardwick is compelled to investigate his suspicious death.

The guy's died. There's a dead body. That's a bit interesting, seeing as I'm a potential mystery reader. I'm listening, but you've killed my interest with the end of that line. What does 'mysterious bystander' even mean? And what's suspicious about ol' Charlie's death?

The third line is the killer.

As Hardwick begins to unravel the mystery, he quickly comes to realise that Charlie Sparks's death throws up more peculiar questions than answers.

Because 'peculiar questions' is going to entice someone to want to read the book, isn't it? If I want peculiar questions, I'll spend half an hour in the company of my son and save myself three quid.

This is a blurb which is going to need some serious work. But that's for another time. We've got a book to write.

WHAT ELSE CAN YOU DO?

Some people perform brilliantly under pressure. I'm one of them, although I don't like having to do it.

Like many people, I'm inherently lazy. If I don't *have* to do something, I probably won't. At the same time, though, if someone tells me I have to do something, I'm even less likely to do it. Indie spirit, and all that.

So I had to take a leap and change my way of thinking about things. One of the changes I made was to take responsibility for my career. Yes, there were things that needed doing, but I made the conscious decision to *want* to do them. I took that external pressure and internalised it, telling myself it was me putting that pressure on myself.

It worked. For me, internal pressure is what fires me. Other people telling me what to do never works. But when I decide I want to take on big projects, they always get done — to a higher standard and in less time than I imagined beforehand.

Perhaps I'm more afraid of letting myself down than I am of letting other people down. Who knows? But the point is I know what works best for me to get things moving and I embrace that, using it to ensure I get things done.

If, for example, you find external pressure works best for you, you might like to set a release date for your book well in advance. Some people set a release date before they've even written a word, and this helps them to actually get it done. It's the external pressure they need to complete the work. After all, if people are expecting it to be ready on a certain date and are already parting with their money for pre-order purchases, what else are you going to do?

I set my own personal deadlines for things, and I always meet them or exceed them. For me, that works. Making those deadlines public and putting external pressure on me would have the opposite effect.

Perhaps you're reading this and thinking that any sort of pressure doesn't work for you. After all, you're a creative, right?

I thought that too. But it turned out that what fired me and got me moving was a different type of pressure — that internal pressure we just spoke about.

But occasionally we all need to take a break.

Sometimes we get overwhelmed and jaded. And that's fine. You're far better taking a rest for a while and coming back at it 100% than you are trying to plod along at 40 or 45%. But keep that internal pressure on, and make sure you don't let yourself down by taking liberties. After all, we can often be our own worst enemies.

SUMMARY — THE INEVITABLE ROADBLOCKS

1. Visualisation can be an extremely powerful tool.
2. Seeing your book's cover can spur you on towards the finish line.
3. Writing the blurb can unlock a new passion for your book.
4. If all else fails, find out what sort of pressure gets you moving.

STAGE 3: PRE-LAUNCH CONSIDERATIONS

It's always worth trying to come up with this when you've got some of the book down, if you haven't already got it.

Book titles will sometimes become apparent through the nature of the story itself. My Knight & Culverhouse books tend to title themselves in this way.

For example, book 3 in the series — *Jack Be Nimble* — is about a copycat killer recreating the grisly murders of Jack the Ripper. It's also the first book in which my main characters' personal lives start to properly unravel and expand, with Jack Culverhouse being one who has some personal demons to face.

Book 6 was entitled *In The Name of the Father*. Not only is it about an insular religious cult, but it's led by Father Joseph Kümmel. It's also the book where Jack Culverhouse's estranged daughter Emily first comes into the series after his wife disappeared with her many years earlier. Jack has to learn how to be a father to her, despite his many personal failings.

Lots of these nuances in the title only become clear once you've read the books, but it just goes to give you an example of how and when the titles become apparent to me.

Some of my books have been far more difficult to title. For example, the titles for *Tell Me I'm Wrong* and *The Perfect Lie* were both chosen from big brainstormed lists my wife and I came up with. Neither of the titles really enthused us, but we felt they were the best of a bad bunch.

When it comes down to it, the title doesn't matter a huge amount. As long as it's evocative of the genre and generates some form of intrigue for the reader, you're on the right track.

KNOWING HOW TO TITLE

Coming up with a book title is an art form in itself. The truth, though, is that your options will be limited by the genre in which you're writing.

Let's have a look at a few titles which are, at the time of writing, in the Kindle charts within certain genres.

Fantasy

Bound by a Dragon
The Dark Huntsman
Angel's Roar
The Lost and the Chosen
Fire and Blood
The Dark Citadel

Note how all those titles seem somehow similar. They all evoke strong mythical or historical thoughts (dragon, huntsman, angel, citadel) and contain strong, mysterious words like 'dark' and 'roar'.

In short, these titles tell you exactly what you're getting. In fact, did you even need me to tell you they were fantasy books?

Let's have a look at another genre.

Crime

Fatal Promise
Hush Hush
Dead If You Don't
Dead Lock
Caught
Only The Innocent

Again, there are recurring themes here. There are two mentions of 'death' and one of 'fatal' in a list of just six randomly selected titles. The others lean towards crime/justice, too (caught, innocent).

Have a look at the top-selling books in your genre and see what tropes and patterns you can spot in the book titles.

SERIES BRANDING

Branding your patterns to your series is something you might want to consider. If you do, you'll want to consider it at the start. There are some benefits and drawbacks you'll need to think about, though.

Doing this can either make it harder for you to title new books (as you'll be constrained by the form you've already created) or it could make it easier (as you've got a starting point and aren't overwhelmed by choice). It really is impossible to tell before you do it.

However, branding your series can definitely help you sell more books, as readers will be even more certain that the books are linked — which will make them want to buy and read more.

Let's have a look at some examples of series titles from different authors:

Peter James (crime)
Dead Simple
Looking Good Dead

Not Dead Enough
Dead Man's Footsteps
Dead Tomorrow

Rachel Caine (fantasy)

Ink and Bone
Paper and Fire
Ash and Quill
Smoke and Iron

Kendall Ryan (romance/erotica)

Misadventures of a City Girl
Misadventures of a Good Wife
Misadventures with my Roommate
Misadventures of a College Girl
Misadventures of a Backup Bride

Sophie Kinsella (women's fiction/romance)

Confessions of a Shopaholic
Mini Shopaholic
Shopaholic & Sister
Shopaholic Abroad
The Secret Dreamworld of a Shopaholic

WHAT IF SOMEONE'S ALREADY USED MY TITLE?

In short, this doesn't matter in the slightest. Book titles cannot be copyrighted.

Let me say that again. **Book titles cannot be copyrighted.**

If you write a book which has the same title as another, tough luck for that author. The same goes if someone does it to you.

There have been a handful of famous cases over the past year or two where authors have tried to claim someone else 'stole' their title. In every case, it's resulted in a huge backlash against the accusing author and has been an absolute PR nightmare for them. Don't be that person. Just don't.

One author even tried to register a word used in her titles as a trademark. That resulted in the entire industry turning against her, and a hugely expensive lawsuit being thrown her way. This isn't the sort of thing you want to be doing.

KEYWORD RESEARCH

First things first, I should mention that this is not a lesson on 'writing to market'. There's a huge difference between positioning your book sensibly in the market and trying to exploit industry trends for commercial gain.

That's not to say that writing to market is a bad idea per se – it's just not the focus of this book, let alone this chapter.

However, you are — presumably — writing your book because you want to sell some copies of it. If that's the case, you need to know who your readers are and what they're looking for when they're seeking a book like yours. After all, if you don't know where and how they're searching, you can't be there to provide them with the prize.

If you've published a book before, you'll probably have noticed the keyword entry box when you were publishing your book to the vendors. Most of them have either one box, a series of boxes or something similar.

Take Amazon KDP, for example — as it's generally considered to be the biggest.

When first entering the details for your new book, you'll see something like this:

There is one bit of text you should take note of there, and one you should ignore. The one you should take note of is the blue link: 'How do I choose keywords?' Clicking this gives you a pop-up with some extra information and a link to a page on Amazon's Help pages entitled **Make Your Book More Discoverable with Keywords**.

This page gives you advice on best practices for using KDP keywords. I quote:

- *Combine keywords in the most logical order. Customers search for "military science fiction" but probably not for "fiction science military"*

• *Use up to seven keywords or short phrases. Keep an eye on the character limit in the text field*

• *Before publishing, search for your book's title and keywords on Amazon. If you get irrelevant or unsatisfying results, make some changes. When searching, look at the suggestions that appear in the "Search" field drop down*

• *Think like a reader. Imagine how you'd search if you were a customer*

It also contains plenty of from-the-horse's mouth advice on what *not* to do, as well as a number of other tips for using the keywords entry boxes to your advantage.

Needless to say, the bit of text on the keyword entry form which should be ignored is the bit which says 'Optional'.

UNLOCKING THE SUBCATEGORIES

Have you ever wondered how books manage to rank in Paranormal Small-Town Cowboy Romance With Goats despite that not being a selectable category in Amazon KDP?

This is largely because of the keywords the author has selected and entered in these seven boxes.

Head over to Amazon KDP's Help pages and

navigate your way through to: *Prepare, Publish, Promote > Publish Your Book > Enter Book Details > Selecting Browse Categories.* There's a section there called *Categories with keyword requirements.*

From there, you can navigate through to your genre(s) and get a flavour of the sorts of keywords you should be using in order to stand a chance of ranking in your relevant categories.

Please note that the specific pages, titles and terminology used in this chapter were correct as of November 2018. It's possible, and likely, that the exact phraseology used by Amazon will change over time, and might not be entirely accurate by the time you read this.

MORE FUN WITH KEYWORDS

Post-launch, your experience with keywords is unlikely to be over. Advertising platforms such as Amazon Advertising (formerly AMS) make great use of custom keywords, and you'll need to find a way of harvesting groups of keywords which your potential readers are likely to be using.

One of my preferred tools for doing so is KDP Rocket. It even has a specific AMS keywords function which will scour Amazon for potentially strong keywords you can use in your advertising campaigns.

Above all else, KDP Rocket can be a fun tool for

analysing what other authors are doing, finding new categories and generally getting under the skin of how Amazon organises and categorises books. I'd recommend downloading it from croft. link/KDPRocket.

Many authors are split on the subject of pre-orders. If you're exclusive to Amazon, then not only are you barking mad but it's also really not worth you doing pre-orders. If you're (sensibly) wide, I'd say they're definitely worth it.

I've experimented with differing lengths of pre-order periods, as well as no pre-order periods at all for a couple of books. The evidence comes down firmly on the side of having pre-orders open, but the jury's still out on length.

WHY PRE-ORDERS ARE A GOOD IDEA

Amazon's a funny old beast in many ways. In other ways, it's actually quite sensible whilst other retailers are a little barmy — but in ways which actually benefit authors.

The world of pre-orders is one such area.

Let's say for argument's sake I've got a book coming out on 1 November and I open it for pre-orders on 1 October. If someone pre-orders the book that day, that counts as a 1 October sale and you get a little rankings boost. If a friend then pre-orders on 4 October, it goes down as a 4 October sale and you get a little rankings boost.

Crucially, neither transaction goes down as a 1 November sale for the purposes of ranking — only in terms of when you get paid for those sales.

The picture gets a little clearer when you look at what the other vendors do.

Let's keep the same hypothetical 1 November release date and 1 October pre-order start date, but this time look at Kobo and Apple.

If someone pre-orders the book on 1 October, it goes down as a 1 October sale and you get a little rankings boost. If a friend then pre-orders on 4 October, it goes down as a 4 October sale and you get a little rankings boost. Same as Amazon, right?

Not quite.

When release day rolls around on 1 November, *all* of your pre-orders then count as 1 November sales *again*. If you've managed to drum up a few hundred pre-orders, that can throw you straight to the top of the charts overnight.

Let's say you get three pre-orders a day at Apple

or Kobo over that month. Three sales a day isn't going to get you charting anywhere particularly impressive. But come 1 November you'll have had 93 pre-orders, and **they will all count cumulatively on release day**.

In effect, you get a double rankings boost from those vendors.

That's why pre-orders are particularly valuable on vendors such as Apple or Kobo, but are pretty useless if you're exclusive to Amazon.

BEWARE THE DEADLINES!

I know, I know. You're an indie and deadlines don't apply to you. But they do when we're talking about pre-orders.

Each vendor has different publishing deadlines when it comes to pre-orders, and you absolutely **must** be aware of them. Failure to adhere to them can result in them stripping your account of pre-order privileges or, in some extreme cases, stopping you from publishing at all.

Each of the vendors has a **maximum pre-order length** — the longest amount of time your book can be on pre-order before release date.

Some also have rules on what you can upload in terms of your **draft**.

They all have a **final draft deadline** in terms of the last day before release that you can make any changes, and before which you must deliver the completed book.

They also all have rules regarding whether or not you can edit your **price** during the pre-order period.

AMAZON KINDLE

Pre-order length: Up to 90 days.

Draft restrictions: None.

Final draft deadline: 3 days (72 hours) before release. The book is then locked and you cannot access it until release.

Pricing: Editable, but not in the final 3 days before release.

APPLE BOOKS

Pre-order length: Up to 1 year.

Draft restrictions: Samples accepted, but no dummy or incomplete files or the book will be ticketed and not go live.

Final draft deadline: 10 days.

Pricing: Editable.

KOBO

Pre-order length: Up to 180 days.

Draft restrictions: At least three chapters.

Final draft deadline: 2 days (48 hours).

Pricing: Editable.

NOOK

Pre-order length: Unclear.

Draft restrictions: None. No placeholder file required either.

Final draft deadline: 3 days (72 hours).

Pricing: Editable.

When it comes to editing pricing, this is not recommended during pre-order periods. To protect customers, most of the main vendors ensure that customers are either guaranteed to pay the price they pre-ordered at, or at the lowest price if it is lowered during the pre-order period.

Make sure you know when these pre-order deadlines are and build them into your pre-release schedule.

FORMATTING YOUR BOOK

If there's one thing which gets overlooked more than anything other by publishers — indie and traditional alike — it's formatting.

In 2017, ebooks accounted for 55% of online book purchases, whereas print books (paperback *and* hardback combined) accounted for just 39% of units sold[1].

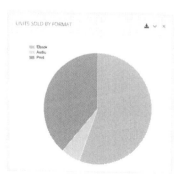

Chart and data courtesy of Author Earnings Report.

As you can see from the chart above, ebooks account for the lion's share of online book purchases. That's nothing new. But let's take a step back.

How much effort do you think goes into typesetting a book for print? Well, for most books it's usually not a whole lot, but many publishers do put a lot of stead in this. I know indie authors do, too. But ebooks — the majority of the market — are often overlooked.

I've truly lost count of the number of books I read on e-readers which look dreadful. It's easily approaching half of all books I read, if not more.

A lot of authors either use only KDP's own online previewer (flawed) or, at most, test their books out on their own Kindle (shortsighted).

I know not everyone can buy every model of e-reader from every company out there (at the time of writing there are five Kobo devices alone), as well as taking care of all the readers who read on mobile devices. But there's a *lot* more authors can do.

Simply loading a Word file into KDP, Kobo Writing Life or iTunes Producer just isn't going to cut the mustard. If you're serious about being an author, you have to respect your readers and put the effort into your finished product.

I wholeheartedly, absolutely and completely recommend you use Vellum[2] to format your books. At the time of writing it's only available to Mac users, but Windows users can use software such as Macin-Cloud to get it working on their PCs.

At first glance, Vellum looks expensive. The price at time of writing is $249.99 for the full version. But let's look at this logically.

Before I used Vellum, I used to get my formatting done by Jason Anderson at Polgarus Studio[3]. Jason's work is excellent, and I still highly recommend him. If you'd prefer to go down that route, Jason's your man — especially if you're only ever going to publish one or two books.

As I write this, having a 100k-word book formatted for ebook and print would cost you $140. By the time you've published two books, it's cost you $280 and buying Vellum will have saved you $30. Each book you publish thereafter saves you $140.

Vellum is only expensive if you're only ever going to publish one book. Once you've published your second, Vellum starts to save you a *lot* of money.

That's not to mention the quality of the books it puts out. Put simply, they're absolutely beautiful, and you can customise the look and feel of your finished book with ease.

Vellum will, at the touch of a button and with no technical expertise required, generate Kindle, Kobo, Apple Books, NOOK, Google Play and generic epub files — as well as paperback files.

Once you've got your paperback formatting sorted, **make sure you order a proof paperback**.

Errors in ebooks can be easily rectified within a few minutes, but you really don't want to be messing around with new editions of paperbacks just to correct a typo or formatting error which could have been spotted in advance.

Now you've got your formatted draft, cover, blurb and a starting point for your marketing, you can get the book off to your editor and pull up your sleeves. It's time to kick things on to the next stage.

---

1. Author Earnings Report, January 2018 (http://authorearnings.com/report/january-2018-report-us-online-book-sales-q2-q4-2017/)
2. https://vellum.pub
3. https://www.polgarusstudio.com

SUMMARY — PRE-LAUNCH CONSIDERATIONS

1. Decide on your book's title, if you don't already have one. By now your book's theme should have become clear, and this task should be easier. You can't go to launch without a title!
2. Research the best keywords to use when submitting your book. This will determine the search pages your book appears on, as well as which subcategory charts it will be eligible for.
3. Consider the pros and cons of pre-orders, and decide on the length and format of your pre-order period — if you choose to do one.
4. Look into formatting options for your book. I highly recommend Vellum, but you

might want to pay someone to format your book by hand.

STAGE 4: PREPARING TO LAUNCH

If you're anything like me, you'll be absolutely useless at keeping your website up to date. Actually, you can't possibly be as bad as me.

Earlier this year, I finally remembered to update my website after my latest book had been out for almost two months. It was only as I was updating it that I realised it didn't even have the *previous* book on it. The most recent book showing on my website was from three books ago.

Again: do as I say, not as I do.

You probably won't sell a huge amount of books through your website. You might not even get much traffic. But it's vital that you respect those readers who do stumble across your site.

An unloved and out-of-date site won't do you any favours. Readers will either think you're not willing to put the effort in or that you're one of those many thousands of authors who tried indie publishing and gave up somewhere along the way.

Many moons ago, in a forgotten age, I used to work in internet marketing. Keeping your website fresh and up-to-date with new content has always been the biggest piece of advice given in that field, and it still holds true today.

Your site needs to look as if it's completely on the ball at all times. Have you been featured on a blog or in a website article? Add it to your site. Perhaps consider adding a blog to show you're still alive.

But make sure you *at least* add a 'coming soon' teaser of your new book, alongside pre-order links to start building up those early sales. And don't forget — pre-order sales at Kobo and Apple Books count double.

TOP TIP

Why not leverage this beautiful little quirk of Kobo and Apple Books by driving your readers towards those platforms?

All Apple devices (iPhones, iPads etc) come with Apple Books installed by default, and users don't need to set up any new accounts. It's literally one tap of a button to buy your book.

Kobo have a free mobile app available for all smartphones and tablets, as well as laptops and PCs. Personally, I think this is the most reliable, beautiful and usable reading app that's ever existed, and it means *everyone* can read Kobo books without buying a new ereader or device.

As an extra aside, and while we're on the topic of your website, you might want to consider making the Apple Books buy button the first one in your list — ahead of Kindle. This is something Apple highly recommend in their guidelines[1] (along with using only approved imagery), and I know for a fact that the folk at Apple actively look at authors' websites and marketing materials to see if they comply. Which authors do you think Apple is going to favour when it comes to new marketing and promotional opportunities?

---

1. https://www.apple.com/itunes/marketing-with-apple-books/identity-guidelines.html

ADD THE BOOK TO YOUR BOOKBUB PROFILE

Once your book is available for pre-order, you should add it to your BookBub profile. (What? You don't have a BookBub profile? Are you mad? Stop reading now and set one up.)

BookBub is the home of voracious readers. It was initially set up as a resource for readers to be alerted to discounted books — either daily or weekly — and BookBub's Featured Deals (often referred to by authors as 'getting a BookBub') still form a core part of its business. However, in more recent times BookBub have noticed the shifting sands in the industry and have shifted their focus to other streams — very sensibly, in my opinion.

Aside from CPM and CPC ads (essentially, paid adverts at the bottom of emails), there is another new addition to the BookBub stable which could prove incredibly useful to you at this stage in your publication process.

NEW RELEASE ALERTS

BookBub will alert readers who follow you on BookBub when you've got a new book out. These people have actively chosen to follow you and get updates on new releases from you, so it's vital you make sure they get it.

Adding your new book to your BookBub profile takes a matter of seconds, and BookBub will do the rest. Once your book is out, they'll send an email to your subscribers (it's free), without any editorial process or gatekeepers (unlike with Featured Deals).

PREORDER ALERTS

Any books with a release date at least eight days in the future, and whose author has over 1,000 followers on BookBub, are eligible for a BookBub Preorder Alert.

If you meet these requirements, I highly recommend setting up a Preorder Alert for your new book.

BookBub will send an email to your followers (at a cost of $0.02 per follower) to let them know about your new book. You can choose the date on which the alert goes out, and it only takes a minute or two to set it up.

CLAIM YOUR BOOK AT AMAZON AUTHOR CENTRAL

Amazon, for some unknown reason, often likes to complicate things.

You can, for example, set your book description in the KDP dashboard, via CreateSpace (no longer in existence) or through Author Central. If your description is slightly different across each of them, there's no telling which one Amazon will decide to use on its product page.

Things get even more confusing when you discover there's a separate Author Central login for each international territory. Why? I don't know. I really don't. Kobo, Apple Books and all the other vendors manage perfectly well to generate author pages from the meta data in your books, so I'm not entirely sure why the biggest book retailer ever to exist seems to struggle so much. But struggle they do, and until they get their stable in order it's just another problem authors have to deal with.

Claiming your book via Amazon Author Central is vital. To do so, you need to head over to author-central.amazon.com. Or .co.uk. Or .ca. Or .com.au. Or… you get the point. It's a ball ache. But it needs doing.

Go to the Books tab, then make sure you've claimed your new title as yours. From there, you can view your book's sales rank and customer reviews — which are about the only things it's useful for, and neither of which are particularly useful anyway.

So why do it? A couple of reasons. Firstly, it stops anyone else claiming your book as theirs. And yes, it has been known. Many times.

Secondly, and most importantly, it means the book is linked to your others on your Amazon author profile. When someone clicks on your author name on an Amazon product listing, it displays the rest of your books. If readers want to find other books by you, this is one of the main ways in which they'll do it, and claiming your book through Author Central more or less guarantees your book will be listed on your profile.

Thirdly, there's always the possibility that Amazon might actually introduce features which capitalise on Author Central's enormous potential.

SERIES LINKING

When adding a new series book to Amazon, make sure the series name is **identical** across all books in the series. To be absolutely certain, copy and paste the series name from one book's KDP entry to the others.

Series linking is huge on Amazon, as it enables readers to know how many books are in a series and gives them an easy way to buy the others.

Here's an example of how it looks on a product page:

Note the series link information just under the star rating.

Clicking on that series link takes readers to a page which lists all the books in that series, complete with 1-Click buy buttons — and even a 1-Click button to buy all the books in the series which the reader doesn't currently own.

This is one area where Amazon is absolutely killing it. It's a brilliant feature, and an opportunity you can't pass up.

Simply adding the series name to your new book will quite often not result in a series link. Keep an eye on your product page, and if the series link doesn't appear within a few days of the pre-order going live, contact Amazon through your KDP dashboard and ask them to enable the series link.

Cliff Richard once sang 'they're wired for sound'. But then again New Musik said 'we're living by numbers', so you can't really trust anyone these days.

Audiobooks are growing. There's no doubt about it. They're still not exploding and taking over the world in the manner in which many industry commentators predict every year, but they're getting there.

I love audio. I really do. I love audiobooks, too. My continual pointing out that growth has actually been relatively slow is not meant to be disparaging about the audiobook industry — far from it. I'm simply pointing out that it's actually been quite disappointing when one considers the huge fanfare it gets.

As we saw earlier, audiobooks had a 6% market share in 2017. At the time of writing, Xiaomi have a

7.26% market share in the worldwide mobile device market. How many of you had heard of them before you read that sentence? Exactly. And they're a bigger player in the enormous swelling behemoth that is the worldwide mobile device market than all audiobooks are in the relatively small online book sales market[1].

Now, I'm not for a minute suggesting that you shouldn't get audiobooks produced. You absolutely should. And there are some very good reasons why.

If you've read *The Indie Author Mindset* you'll know I'm all about the long term. Audiobooks are expensive to produce, but they'll bring in money every month (hopefully) for a long time (hopefully).

It's a bit like having a pension. You pay the money in, knowing you'll get it back numerous times over at some point in the future. And, if audio does ever have the big boom that's been predicted every year for the last ten, we'll all be quids in.

If you write non-fiction, audio is even more of a no-brainer. I mentioned in *The Indie Author Mindset* that I was predicting the audiobook of that title would do better than my fiction. I was right. It now regularly sells more copies in audio than all of my other books put together — and there's nearly twenty of them.

Audiobooks, per copy sold, will likely earn you a far higher royalty than your ebooks or paperbacks, too. You can't set the price for your audiobooks, though — or at least not through ACX, Amazon's audiobook creation platform. Instead, they set the price of your audiobook according to its length.

That means that books which are longer will fall into a higher price bracket, and will therefore give the author a larger royalty per audiobook sold. So, the longer your book is, the more money you'll earn.

Once you've got your first draft written, I'd recommend going to ACX or Findaway Voices and putting your audiobook out to audition.

Of course, your narrator can't start work until you've finalised your book because it needs to be identical to the published version for things like Whispersync to work. And you want Whispersync to work.

In effect, anyone buying the Kindle edition of your book can add on the audiobook either for free or for a small cost. Where things get *really* funky is when you're reading *and* listening to the book.

Using a Kindle (or the Kindle mobile app) you can read a book, then lock your Kindle, jump in the car and put the audiobook on. The audiobook will start playing from the point where you finished reading on your Kindle earlier. When you get out the car later and go back inside to read, your Kindle will have skipped on to the point where you switched the audiobook off.

That's Whispersync in action, and it's **brilliant**. Why Amazon don't make more of it is an absolute mystery to me. Most readers I speak to don't know about it, and the majority of writers aren't aware of its power either. But a lot of audiobooks you sell will be Whispersync add-ons, and these can be the bread and butter of your audiobook income.

---

1. That paragraph has a lot of uses of the word 'market'. It's a bit like when you say a word too many times and it completely loses its meaning. Market market market. Market. Market market. Market. See? Like that.

LAUNCH PARTIES

I'm conflicted when it comes to launch parties.

I don't consider them to be a vital or necessary part of a book launch, but there's no denying they can be fun and do have their uses.

I organised my own launch party for the 2016 release of *In the Name of the Father*, my sixth Knight & Culverhouse book, in which an enigmatic pastor creates a death cult on the outskirts of Mildenheath with the endgame of ritual mass suicide. Just the sort of thing that requires a party.

It was good fun, but it was a lot of work and I wasn't convinced it did a whole lot of good.

In essence, it was a day-long series of events on my Facebook page, which at the time had around 20,000 members. There were clips of me reading extracts from the books, competitions to win signed paperbacks and e-readers, live videos and all sorts of fun and frivolity.

Net benefit result? Not a whole lot. But it did have some considerable upsides.

The feedback I got from readers was that it made them feel involved in the book launch process, and that it brought me closer to them. That is the sort of thing you can't put a value on. That event turned casual readers into lifelong fans. It's all part of the overall 'halo effect'.

That said, I didn't do another launch party until the 2018 release of *The Perfect Lie*, and that was mainly because I'd recently hired a new PA and she was adamant a launch party would be beneficial.

This time, it was just a couple of hours in the evening (UK time), and consisted of me doing a couple of live videos as well as appearances by guest authors, who 'took over' my Facebook page for half an hour at a time to talk about their books and answer questions from my readers.

Again, it opened things up and made the whole process much more personal.

That said, launch parties are a lot of work to organise. The logic underpinning trying to be more personable and forging long-term relationships with readers is sound. That is something I am absolutely, 100% firmly behind. But I think there might be less labour-intensive ways of doing it.

Having said that, launch parties are fun. If you

fancy organising one, I recommend hosting it on your Facebook page or group (which you *really* should have). Facebook's a social gathering place and is used by most people, so doesn't require any sort of learning curve for readers.

Set your date, let your mailing list (and Facebook fans) know, change your header graphic to promote the launch party and get planning.

Here are a few things you could do:

- **Live videos.** These work really well on Facebook. It allows your readers to interact with you live, and gives you an immediate, personal presence rather than something pre-produced.
- **Competitions and giveaways.** Signed paperback editions of your new book always go down well, as do full libraries of all your existing work in ebook form.
- **Exclusive readings.** These can be done using live video, or can be pre-recorded and posted to the page on launch day.
- **Guest author appearances.** This shows it's not all about you, but that you want to promote great books in general. It's also a nice thing to do and gives validity to your book launch that other authors are getting involved with it.

SUMMARY — PREPARING TO LAUNCH

1. Ensure your website is updated with the new book.
2. Strongly consider the vendors' guidelines on styling your promotional copy.
3. Claim your book at Amazon Author Central in each relevant territory.
4. Ensure your book is series linked if necessary.
5. Put your book up for audiobook audition.
6. Consider a launch party for increasing reader engagement and awareness.

STAGE 5: THE LAUNCH

LAUNCH STRATEGIES

By now, you'll be thinking about your launch strategy. If you're not, you should be.

That's not to say that I think just quietly releasing a book and working your way from there isn't a solid plan — it totally is.

There are a few ways of looking at launch strategies, and each of them has its own benefits and drawbacks.

THE BIG BUILDUP

This is the oft-touted style of book launch in the indie world, and one which certainly has some benefits, but it also has some pretty significant drawbacks.

In effect, this strategy consists of having a pre-order period of at least a month, during which time you send out emails to your mailing list, get book bloggers on board, hammer social media and run all manner of paid ads to build up buzz for your book ahead of release.

This strategy has its roots in the traditional publishing world, where books have a shelf life. If a traditionally published book doesn't sell like hotcakes in its first week or two, it's yanked from the shelves and pulped, ready to make way for the next title the publishers have banked all their hopes on.

In the digital world, and in the indie market, that just isn't a *thing*. Once your book is out, it's out. It doesn't have a shelf life. It doesn't come off sale. It's always available for readers to buy, whether in digital or in print.

This model does have benefits, of course. Large pre-order sales can bring you huge success on platforms such as Apple Books and Kobo (where pre-orders count twice, remember) and give you enormous launch day spikes which will propel you to the top of the charts overnight.

However, charts aren't anywhere near as important as they used to be. They're more difficult to find on the iOS version of Apple Books since it was rebranded in 2018 and Kobo does a brilliant job of keeping its charts pretty well hidden.

There are very good reasons why retailers do this nowadays. Primarily it's because they've done testing and they know what works. **And they know charts don't sell books**.

In the modern market, books are sold far more successfully through algorithms that suggest books a reader is likely to enjoy based on their past reading and browsing experiences.

In short, having a launch strategy based on a primary (or even secondary) target of chart positions is somewhat misguided and outdated in the modern publishing industry.

That's not to say this approach doesn't work, though. Retailers such as Apple Books and Kobo very much look at the strength of a book's pre-release period and will put forward successful or 'hot' books for additional promotions and marketing opportunities which aren't available elsewhere.

A note on Amazon, though. Although Amazon are notoriously tight-lipped about their algorithms, there's a lot of documentary evidence to support the suggestion that sales spikes will do you more harm than good on their platform.

Apple Books, for example, appears to have its charts and ranking algorithm based not only on sales, but also on 'hits' to your book's product page.

Amazon's ranking algorithm, on the other hand, is actually pretty simple and crude in the modern industry, and is all about the sheer number of units shifted, with a slight skew towards recent historical data (the previous day's sales supposedly count half, the day previous to that by a factor of 25% and so forth). Amazon is about stability of sales, and big spikes can harm you. That's why things like BookBub Featured Deals aren't as good for Amazon as they used to be.

THE 'HIT AND HOPE'

These are terms I'm pretty much making up on the spot, by the way. But you're all *totally* going to use them all the time and make me sound like some sort of visionary, right? Right?

The 'hit and hope' method is something I've used before, and it hasn't worked particularly well for me. It certainly has its merits, though.

This is the method a lot of first-time authors use, and in that situation it can certainly be a good way to do things.

It involves putting the book live when it's ready — without a pre-order period — and then slowly gearing up your marketing efforts.

If you're a new author publishing your first book, this can certainly be less daunting and it can also have other benefits. By slowly building your marketing efforts and sales, you're going to get some valuable early feedback from your first readers which could be vital to helping you polish your book and tweak it before gearing up with larger marketing efforts.

I tried this approach for a book very recently, in 2017, with my book *With a Vengeance*. I wanted to see what difference it would make to sales in the long and short term to not bother with a pre-order period or any pre-launch fuss.

In the short term, it was pretty horrendous. I've got a huge fanbase now, so I know if I put a book up for pre-order I'm pretty much guaranteed pre-orders in the thousands. Using this approach, of course, I got no pre-orders whatsoever as there wasn't a pre-order available.

A year and a half on, though, and it doesn't appear to have harmed the book in the long-term.

It was book 7 in my Knight & Culverhouse series, so I'm looking at it compared to books 6 and 8, both of which had pre-order periods of around a month.

As I write this, book 7 has sold almost a third as many copies as book 6, but three and a half times as many as book 8. That's not too surprising, as it's been on the shelves a year less than book 6 and a year longer than book 8. Readers also tend to read the books in order, so the sales numbers of later books will be lower while readers are catching up.

To clarify, in terms of units sold, book 7 sold 30% of what book 6 did and 350% of what book 8 did. But when you look at the money they've each earned, the picture is slightly different.

Book 7 has earned 76% of what book 6 has, and 146% of what book 8 has. In other words, the money each of the books has earned me is actually very similar, and almost identical when you take into account the amount of time each has been out.

WHY IS THIS?

Put simply, it's because I tried different launch approaches for each book.

For book 6, I did a pre-order period during which my mailing list subscribers were given a 50% discount off the launch price. I did this by putting the book up for pre-order at £1.99/$2.99, then raising the price on release day.

For book 7, I went straight to launch at full price.

For book 8, I took a similar approach to book 6, but with a 25% pre-order discount.

The key takeaway here, though, is that **it made absolutely no difference in the long run**.

As should be expected, the big discounts shifted more units but returned a lower revenue and the full-price launch shifted fewer units but returned a higher revenue.

Let's have a look at how each book did in its first year on sale.

Book 6, *In the Name of the Father*, was the one for which my mailing list were given a 50% pre-order discount. Let's call that the benchmark — so revenue earned is 100%.

Book 7, *With A Vengeance* was the book which

went straight to market at full price. Compared to book 6, book 7 made 87.7% as much revenue.

Book 8, *Dead & Buried*, was the one that had a 50% pre-order discount for my mailing list. It's only five months old at the time of writing, but has currently made 66.7% of the money book 6 did in its first year.

Still with me? If you're not, the figures are still showing that there's not a *huge* difference in the long-term effect of different launch approaches, but that a pre-order period and mailing list discount seems to help.

If you are still with me, let's make the data super accurate and account for book 8 only being five months old, and compare the first five months of each book being on sale.

Book 6 is our benchmark, so in its first five months earned 100% of revenue.

Compared to that, book 7, with no pre-order period and straight to full price earned 78.9% as much revenue as book 6 over the same time period.

Book 8, for which there was a 25% pre-order discount (compared to book 6's 50%) earned 92.6% as much in its first five months on sale, compared to book 6.

In short, pre-order periods work and discounting your books during the pre-order period for your mailing list also works. A 50% discount will earn you more money in the long run (8% higher revenues after five months) by my figures.

A note of caution, though. My mailing list was significantly larger for book 8 than it was for book 6. To do a thorough test, my next two books in that series will be launched with a 25% discount for one book, and no discount but a pre-order period of around a month on the other. That will give us a more comprehensive set of data moving forward.

MY LAUNCH APPROACH

I've been publishing for a long time now, and I've got a lot of readers who've stuck with me right from the start. My mailing list is my biggest business tool by a long way, so I'm always extremely keen to reward people who are on it.

As a result, I put my new books up on pre-order for a month or so at a discounted price, then raise it on release day. Before release, I market only to my mailing list and social media channels. It's my hard-core, dedicated fans who I want to get the discount. It's my 'thank you' to them.

Then, once the book is out and up at full price, I start the wider marketing.

I find this approach rewards my loyal readers and also enables me to make a full royalty on sales to new readers. This is important, as I then know those new readers are ones willing to pay the retail price for a book. I'm not simply filling my mailing list with bargain hunters. They will, however, be rewarded with discounts and bargains when new books are released. It's win-win.

As for the level of discount I offer, as you can see from the stats above, I've tried different approaches. The jury's still out on what works best, and in any case it's likely to differ from genre to genre.

BOOK BLOGGERS

I love book bloggers. Most authors do.

As I write this, I'm reminded of a recent episode in which a minor publisher went off on a bizarre Twitter rant about how useless book bloggers are.

This particular publisher is notorious for trying to be gobby as a publicity stunt in an attempt to sell books. His company accounts show his approach definitely doesn't work, with his company spiralling in debt, which is almost doubling year on year, and failing to turn a profit in four years. I know a few authors who've been with this publisher, and none of them have a good word to say about him.

Put simply, the chap hasn't got a clue what he's talking about.

Book bloggers are awesome people who take the time to read our books, blog their reviews and share the book love all over social media. I know *for a fact* that book bloggers drive book sales, because I've had countless readers emailing me to tell me they've discovered my books after reading a review on a blog.

The book blogging community is huge. The blogging community full-stop is huge.

When I say 'bloggers', I'm talking about all online influencers. Largely, that extends to physical bloggers, YouTubers and Instagrammers. In other industries, companies pay these influencers huge amounts of money to endorse their products. Fortunately, the book industry hasn't quite reached that level of crassness, but has — I believe — found a good balance which indie authors can use to their advantage.

Word of mouth is the strongest form of marketing. That's always been true. Having a company or product recommended by a family member or friend is always going to be the most compelling advert.

But in today's interconnected online world, social media friends and personalities tend to fall into more or less the same sphere. They're trusted people, and readers follow their reviews and social media postings to get an idea of which books they might like.

What's more, the bloggers usually don't charge for the service. You'll usually have to get in touch with them well in advance and book a slot for them to read and review your book, so this is something you'll need to think about early on in your planning process. I've included it here, though, as it's also a more than viable marketing strategy for backlist books and following a release.

For instance, I tend to send my books to book bloggers quite late. That's usually because I put my book up for pre-order before it's even finished, and am usually making tweaks and edits right up until deadline day. As a result, many book bloggers only get round to reading my book after it's been released. But that's absolutely fine. In fact, it's more than fine.

These reviews can provide a nice injection of sales and new readers weeks down the line, once the initial launch buzz has worn off and sales would otherwise start to dip. It's a very handy way of avoiding the notorious (and, in my opinion, fictional) thirty-day cliff (a popular but largely unfounded perception that Amazon somehow — and for some reason — 'punishes' books arbitrarily once they reach thirty days old, for no reason whatsoever) and plays right into the hands of the slow and steady launch strategy I spoke about in the last chapter.

Regardless of what the aforementioned slightly barmy publisher says, book bloggers are widely regarded as a hugely valuable resource, and should certainly form a part of your overall marketing strategy.

FINDING BOOK BLOGGERS

Lots of authors tell me they find it difficult to find book bloggers to contact. That strikes me as odd, because I've certainly never found there to be a shortage. In fact, I'm fairly sure I've got at least five hiding under my stairs. Every time I open a cupboard to fetch the teabags — there we are, another book blogger.

Okay, so maybe they're not quite that abundant, but they're not far off. And why wouldn't they be? Think about it for a moment. These guys *love* books. Blogs are free and easy to set up, and as a result they can enjoy tons of free books, sent to them by the authors, in return for an honest and unbiased review on their website. They get to feed their addiction at no cost; authors get valuable word-of-mouth promotion. Everyone's a winner.

Most book bloggers are prominent on social media, too. Blogs aren't satellite sites which just exist in the ether; they need social media to drive traffic towards them. If social media is the café or bar where everyone's talking about what they love, blogs are the 'come back here a sec and take a look at this'.

The primary social media outlets for finding book bloggers (purely because they're the easiest and most abundant platforms) are Twitter and Instagram.

On Twitter, you can literally just search 'book blogger' in the search field, then surf through the results or hop through the 'Similar Users' feature to find more people. Follow any bloggers who appear to review books in your genre or niche.

On Instagram, you want to be looking at hashtags. Some of the most popular ones are #bookstagram and #bookblogger. By looking at the other hashtags users are putting on their posts there, you'll be able to navigate your way through other viable hashtags for your books and genre.

APPROACHING BOOK BLOGGERS

I've been very fortunate to get to know some of the best book bloggers in the business. I figured, rather than me trying to give you advice on how to approach them, it'd be best to ask them directly what they're looking for when deciding which new books to review.

I think communication is key. Not only about the obvious such as date of publication but what the book is about (honestly).

Most bloggers have preferred genres and hence need to perhaps know more than just "the blurb". Getting posters or any amendments in plenty of time and getting the book to them at least a month before publication is also a must wherever possible.

We can occasionally fit in last minute things but

not too many as we often get lots of asks, some of which are not always possible.

It's nice to have a social media relationship but perhaps not with every author as we get spammed and sent book links too often otherwise, so I think we prefer to pick and choose who we are friends with.

An author having a good social media platform does help us to see what they are like, as well as about their books.

NICKI MURPHY, NICKI'S BOOK BLOG

A lot of top rated book bloggers on Goodreads and Amazon are quite busy and never at a loss for something to read.

I work with several authors whose books I get several months before they are published. Personally, this works for me because if an author wants reviews on or around publication date they can be assured I'll meet that.

Give me a couple of weeks and I'd have to refuse.

Just give me it with spelling mistakes. I'm okay with that. Yes, let me read the edited version but I'm happy to read an ARC and take it on its story and not the spelling or grammar.

Professional reviewers won't merit it on

spelling mistakes as they know it's a proof read. They merit the story.

But an author needs to do their research about a blogger. It's no good asking someone to read a fantasy book if all they read are thrillers.

Approaching a blogger is difficult, but as long as the author knows a little about the blogger they are approaching it should be fine.

It's okay to ask a blogger kindly when you think your book will be read. Sometimes we forget or it gets pushed down. Most of us do not have TBR piles; we have mountains!

Please share the bloggers' efforts. It makes their day when a little appreciation is shown.

Don't email and say 'I saw you liked such and such book, I think you'll like mine!' A lot of bloggers hate comparing books. If I liked that one, what makes you think I'll like yours?

SUE WARD, READ ALONG WITH SUE

First, I have to mention reviews. I don't charge for reviews. Never have and never will, and neither will the majority of bloggers. There is no integrity to a paid review and it is against Amazon rules and probably many other retailers. Some bloggers do charge, and I am often shocked to hear how much. In my opinion reviews should be unbiased and therefore free and authors shouldn't pay for one.

It is helpful, and more beneficial to both parties, if you check what genres the blogger usually reads. My preferred genre is crime fiction, but I do read other genres.

It is always nice to have some kind of relationship with the author I am helping, so I would recommend building some kind of relationship first. I have been sent a friend request and upon accepting I then receive a message 'Hello, thank you for accepting my friend request. I am attaching a review copy of my book'. I am afraid to me that looks as though you only want to be my friend so that you can get a review. It will probably just get you blocked and/or unfriended.

From experience these are few and far between, but I have been asked to review a book and when I decline for whatever reason (usually because I am backed up with books to review) I receive a response something like 'that is a shame because you are missing out on the best debut out there'. Anything along those lines will probably receive a reply along the lines of: 'If it is the best debut out there then you don't need me'. I am afraid I don't have much patience with authors who think they are better than any other author I have agreed to help. On the whole, however, I have found authors tend to all help and support one another and in turn we help where we can.

If you are requesting a review, a friendly

message along with a synopsis and the number of pages will give us an idea of how much time is needed and if the book is one we would enjoy. If we have the time and are interested, that is the time to send the book and agree a timeframe.

The main thing to take on board is that if I don't like a book, that doesn't mean it isn't a brilliant book — just that it isn't for me. Some people like the traditional detective books where the focus is on the investigation, whereas I like psychological thrillers and the more blood, gore and evilness the better. Looking at what the blogger has read in the past is always useful. Goodreads is an excellent tool for this purpose. That said, I also enjoy historical fiction, so it is always worth contacting me on the offchance.

Finally, publishing is seasonal and there are times of year when books are flying in from all angles, so you are more likely to get a review if you try to aim for the quieter periods.

Don't get disheartened. There are a lot of bloggers and readers. Keep asking. Someone somewhere will be willing and able to help. Also try Facebook groups. Some will allow you to post requesting a review or ask on your behalf, but check the group rules first.

JILL BURKINSHAW, BOOKS N ALL

PAID ADVERTISING

I'll say it now: this chapter will not have any juicy tips or strategies for Facebook ads, BookBub ads or AMS ads. If you've skipped to this chapter in the hope of a quick fix, I'm sorry to disappoint you.

Let me explain.

People often ask me to write a book on marketing — specifically on paid advertising, such as Facebook ads. That's something I won't do, and can't do. There are two main reasons why.

Firstly, what works and what doesn't work changes quickly and often. By the time I've written a book on what works, a large amount of it won't work anymore. After two months, the book would be completely redundant. That's why I tend to share these sorts of tips and tricks in my Facebook group, so I can keep the advice current, true and useful.

Secondly, what works for me will likely not work

for you. There are, of course, strategies and pieces of advice that hold true for the vast majority of people, but slavishly copying what I do is extremely unlikely to do you any benefit.

In fact, my strategies usually don't work for me. I've tried copying the same principles from my ads for my most successful two books (each of which has earned me profits significantly into six figures) across to my other books, and it hasn't worked.

I've had two extremely successful Facebook ads campaigns — with *Her Last Tomorrow* and the even more popular *Tell Me I'm Wrong* — but they're just two of twenty-four titles I have out at the time of writing. That's an 8.3% hit rate.

Don't get me wrong — that 8.3% hit rate has completely changed my life, transformed my career and sent everything stratospheric, but statistically I've still failed at Facebook ads 91.7% of the time. And that's all while using my own advice and my own successful strategies, too.

In short, if my advice fails *me* 91.7% of the time, I'm really not comfortable advising you to follow my lead.

Facebook advertising *does* work. Of course it does. I'm the poster boy for that fact. But it's what works for *you* that counts.

There are a few types of paid online advertising I use, and I'm going to run you through the main ones here.

FACEBOOK

There's no getting away from it – Facebook is huge. It's a brilliant way to reach a large audience of potential readers, but it does have its drawbacks.

One of the things that makes it tricky to advertise on Facebook is that users aren't there to be sold to. This is, of course, changing as Facebook users get more used to seeing adverts on the platform, but it's still a hurdle which must be overcome.

For more information on how to use Facebook advertising in depth, I'd strongly recommend Mark Dawson's Ads for Authors course.

It's no secret that Facebook advertising is becoming more difficult and more expensive due to the number of advertisers now exploiting the platform. It is also a commonly held belief that the life cycle of a Facebook advert is often only a matter of weeks, if not a couple of months, and that users quickly become desensitised to your ads, which will need revamping and revitalising often.

Seasonality can also be a huge issue with Facebook advertising. It goes without saying that more people will be advertising around the time of Christmas, for example, but many authors misunderstand how this competition works.

When you're bidding to have your advert shown to Facebook users, you're not just competing with other authors. Those Facebook users are also being targeted by companies selling cars, fitness equipment, home gadgets and all sorts of other products.

Our industry involves very small margins. We really can't afford for CPCs to rise much above $0.20 if we are advertising a book on which the royalty is, for example, $2.50. However, a company selling a home gadget on which their markup is fifty or sixty dollars can afford to pay much higher CPCs and still turn a profit.

Nowadays, though, it's not just new users and potential readers that you need to pay to reach on Facebook. Facebook has moved the goalposts, ensuring that you now need to pay in order to reach your own fans.

It's been the case for a while now that Facebook Pages have enjoyed far less organic visibility than they used to. Facebook is all about keeping users on the platform, and using their newsfeed. It prioritises showing users posts which have high levels of engagement. If you don't have that high level of engagement on posts from your author page, you might find it difficult to reach your own audience.

For Pages, Facebook now recommends boosting your posts. This is relatively inexpensive and does allow you to get your posts visible, but it does stick in the throat somewhat. It's understandable, though, as Facebook relies solely on advertising revenues in order to function.

For a while, some people recommended using

Facebook Groups as opposed to Pages in order to get around this, but it seemed obvious to me that Facebook would soon close this loophole, and that the work of setting up these groups would be null and void within a short matter of time. Only recently, in fact, it is been announced that Facebook has done just that.

That isn't to say that Groups are useless. Far from it. The levels of engagements in Groups are generally much higher than on Pages, which will tend to give your Group posts much more natural visibility.

AMAZON ADVERTISING

Until recently, these were known as AMS Ads. Amazon Advertising is Amazon's proprietary paid ads system. It allows authors to have their adverts shown on the product pages for other books, as well as search results pages and some other locations on the Amazon website.

The potential for this, as you might well imagine, is huge. Unlike Facebook, users on Amazon's website will usually be actively looking to buy a book. Because Amazon is a retail website, users will almost certainly be looking to buy *something*.

However, Amazon Advertising is not without its significant drawbacks. Reporting is famously dreadful compared to other online advertising platforms, with the dashboard being far from live. In fact, it often takes days – if not weeks – for the dashboard to update. This makes it almost impossible to determine whether or not your ads are working.

Amazon Advertising also suffers from issues regarding scalability. It's actually remarkably difficult to get Amazon to spend your money. Simply increasing the budget quite often does nothing, and more often than not can kill a previously successful ad.

There are far better qualified people than me who can advise in more detail about Amazon Advertising, including Brian Meeks, but it appears that this is one area in which users in KDP Select enjoy a slight advantage. This is primarily because Kindle Unlimited subscribers can effectively get your book for 'free', and you'll still be paid a (small) royalty if they read the book.

BOOKBUB ADS

It's worth mentioning from the beginning, that BookBub Ads are different from BookBub Featured Deals and other BookBub products.

This particular platform is CPM/CPC based in much the same way as Facebook and Amazon Advertising. Contrary to Amazon Advertising, though, BookBub Ads don't actually work particularly well for selling books on Amazon.

Where they really come into their own, though, is

in helping you sell books on the other vendors. They are particularly useful when it comes to selling books on Apple Books, Kobo and NOOK.

Some people using this platform get hung up over things which matter far less than they do on other platforms. For example, CTR (click through rate) is often quoted as a measure of success, whereas in reality it's actually fairly meaningless.

It's also well worth mentioning that your CPCs can be quite a bit higher on BookBub than other advertising platforms, and you will still be able to turn a decent profit. This is because your ad will be shown in emails alongside Featured Deals, to an audience which is already primed and ready to buy books. This means that the percentage of users who will click your ad and *not* buy the book is much lower.

Contrary to popular belief, BookBub users are not just after bargains. The company's own continual studies show that the vast majority of their users also buy full-price books.

KOBO PROMOTIONS

Kobo Promotions are a hugely valuable marketing tool, but are largely overlooked by the majority of authors — even many of those who publish through Kobo.

The main reason for this is that the Promotions

tab is not open to all authors by default. It's technically still in testing mode, but can be unlocked by emailing writinglife@kobo.com and asking them to grant you access to the Promotions tab.

Once it's unlocked, you'll be able to apply for promotions through your Kobo Writing Life dashboard.

I find the ones which work best for me are the % off or x for y deals. Some of the most popular deals of this type are 40% off or 3 for 2. But why are they so great?

Firstly, they're the sorts of offers shoppers recognise. They look great. '40% off' sounds better than '£3.99 reduced to £2.39'.

Secondly, the discounts are applied at the checkout, so Amazon never sees your book at its discounted price and won't try price matching it. That means you can make the deals exclusive to Kobo without worrying about other vendors cannibalising your royalties.

That said, price-drop promos (in which you actively drop the book's price for a set period of time during the promotion) can also be extremely valuable. I'd advise trying all forms of Kobo promotion that match your genre of book and seeing what works best for you.

PRE-LAUNCH PAID ADVERTISING TIPS

The sort of paid advertising you should be doing pre-launch depends entirely on what sort of launch you've planned.

If you've got your book up for discounted pre-order, this is worth mentioning in your ad copy. Phrases such as 'limited time only', 'discounted' and 'exclusive' can work very well across many different advertising platforms.

BookBub Ads, for example, respond very well to words such as 'free', 'cheap' and 'new' used within the imagery.

Of course, if your book is discounted in the pre-order period, it's worth remembering that your royalty per copy sold will be lower. To that effect, you should either advertise your book only to people you know will buy (your mailing list, Facebook Page 'likes' or social media followers) or accept that your advertising campaign is for visibility rather than profit.

At this point, I should mention that some marketing and advertising platforms can be merged or cross-utilised in some interesting and powerful ways.

For example, you can create a Custom Audience on Facebook based on your mailing list. This will enable you to fire Facebook ads at members of your mailing list, making sure they definitely know about your new release. After all, what percentage of your mailing list never open your emails? And of those who do, how many simply forget or put it off until later?

As part of your long-term advertising and marketing strategy for your new book, you should consider and plan which types of readers you want to reach at which point in the launch cycle.

For example, I begin by advertising to my mailing list through Mailchimp. I will also use boosted posts from my Facebook Page and run Facebook ads to a Custom Audience of my mailing list members. This ensures that everyone who's actively signed up to hear from me has the best chance of finding out about my new book.

While we're on the subject of mailing lists, let's have a look at them in a little more detail.

MAILING LIST LAUNCH STRATEGIES

There are a number of different methods authors use when it comes to promoting their new releases to their mailing lists. I've tried many different strategies myself. But I've found the old, tried and tested methods still seem to work best.

It's true to say that books are impulse purchases. When it comes to readers buying books from authors they already know and love, though, it's a little bit different.

For me, the following strategy always tends to work well. I should mention, though, that some steps in the mailing list strategy should be taken earlier in the launch process — some as early as Stage 1 or 2. They'll be marked on the final checklist at the end of the book.

STEP 1: THE TEASER

The first mention of any new book to my mailing list is usually fairly minor. I might casually mention in an email that my next book is nearly finished. I might even hint as to which series its in, or whether it's a standalone book.

This is enough to have a large number of readers replying to me and asking for more information. At that point, I'll let them know a bit more. No titles, covers or plots, but something extra to what was in the original email.

> **Top tip:** Any emails you send which elicit some sort of response from the reader are gold dust. One of the measures email providers use for determining spammers is to look at the level of interaction and response to emails.
>
> If lots of your subscribers respond to you or interact with your emails in some way, you'll get much higher deliverability rates in future.
>
> This is crucial. When you've got a new book out, the difference between 20% of your subscribers opening the email and 40% opening the email is *not* 20% — it's 100% more.
>
> A jump in deliverability from 20% to 40% would, in effect, double your sales from your newsletter.

STEP 2: THE COVER REVEAL

For most of my readers, this will be the first time they really sit up and take notice.

Graphics are a great way to grab people's attention, and a new book cover is guaranteed to stand out to a reader.

> **Top tip:** It's worth being careful when it comes to images in emails. Too many, and it'll appear obvious to email filters that it's a newsletter and your deliverability rates will drop.

As opposed to the earlier tease about this mythical, ethereal new book, the cover reveal makes it real. It's now an actual book, with an actual cover, and is actually happening. Cue reader excitement.

STEP 3: THE BLURB REVEAL

This third email is similar to Step 2, but contains the blurb or teaser about the book's content. This is where you really hook the reader in and make them want this book *now*. Except they can't have it now. You're such a good person, though, that there is a little something you will do for them.

But they'll have to wait until your next email to find out…

STEP 4: THE 'COME AND GET IT'

By now, your readers will be frothing at the mouth and rubbing their upper thighs whilst crouching slightly. Probably.

This is where you drop the call to action.

Once the book's up and available for pre-order, get those links out to your readers — as well as mentioning their pre-order discount if you're doing one — and encourage them to pre-order their copy now.

STEP 5: THE FIRST CHAPTER

Giving your readers a small part of the book for free, as a teaser, is a great way to generate more interest and build up pre-order buzz amongst your mailing list.

It's worth mentioning that this doesn't need to be the first chapter in a physical sense: it can be any chapter, or any snippet from your book. You just need to make sure it's the *right* snippet.

Make sure you end on some sort of cliffhanger — something which makes the reader feel they *have* to buy the book and find out what happens. And, of course, don't forget to include the pre-order links.

STEP 6: THE 'NO, SERIOUSLY, COME AND GET IT'

By now you've sent five emails. You've also sent them the links and a call to action. If they haven't bought it now, they never will — right?

Wrong.

Take my latest book release, for example — *The Perfect Lie*. A week before the book was released, I sent a reminder email about pre-orders. Bear in mind the book was up for pre-order for a month, and this was — I think — the *third* pre-order notice subscribers had. A stunning 837 people clicked the pre-order link in that email, despite having had six or seven emails about the book in total and three emails with pre-order links. Why? Because the deadline was looming, and this was almost their last chance…

STEP 7: THE LAST CHANCE

This might seem like it's getting a bit silly now, but it's necessary. Trust me.

Don't assume everyone's opening all your emails and taking it all in. They get lots of emails from lots of people and they *will* forget.

Maybe they opened the email at work or while they were in the middle of something and filed it in the 'I'll look at this later' section of their brain. I do it all the time. I know you do, too. Everyone does.

Some people don't even notice I've got a new

book out until the third *after*-launch email, despite me being able to see they opened and read them all.

So, never assume anything.

Let's look at my last launch, again, for *The Perfect Lie*. One day before release, I sent a 'This is your last chance!' email about pre-orders. I told them the price was going up in a few hours, so they'd better grab it now. Despite all the emails I already sent about the book, 986 people clicked the pre-order links in that email.

Yeah. I know.

STEP 8: THE THANK YOU

A few days after each release, I email my list to let them know how launch day went, how successful the book has been and share some pictures of chart positions. Readers love to feel involved with things like this, and to feel they've made a contribution.

I thank them for buying the book and ask them to leave a review on the site they bought it from once they've read it.

I also include buy links for anyone who — somehow — didn't pre-order the book and hasn't bought it already.

When I did this after releasing The Perfect Lie, a whopping 534 people clicked the buy links for the book, despite it now being double the price and them having received multiple emails about the book with buy links in each of them.

Never assume you've got the message across.

But how often should you be sending these emails?

That all depends on how long your launch process is. My pre-order periods last a month or so, so my email schedule looks a little like this:

Launch + 5 days: Step 8: The thank you
Launch -1 day: Step 7: The last chance
Launch -7 days: Step 6: The 'no, seriously, come and get it'
Launch -14 days: Step 5: The first chapter
Launch -30 days: Step 4: The 'come and get it'
Launch -45 days: Step 3: The blurb reveal
Launch -60 days: Step 2: The cover reveal
At some point before then: Step 1: The teaser

Please bear in mind that this is only the way I personally do things. You might well find a different schedule works better for you. I, for one, will be experimenting with different schedules for my future books and have used different schedules in the past.

DISCOUNT PROMO SITES

In the early-ish days of digital publishing, discount promo sites used to be absolutely huge.

BookBub Featured Deals are the largest and best-known of these promos, and they can still be a powerful weapon in the author's arsenal.

The usual format is that readers will subscribe to be notified of discounted books on a daily or weekly basis. Authors apply to have their book included (and pay for doing so), then discount their book on the agreed day.

Generally speaking, these don't work as well as they used to. BookBub Featured Deals, for example, will usually cost four figures for a one-day promotion. They used to be absolutely guaranteed to turn a profit — usually trebling or quadrupling your outlay — but are less valuable nowadays. For new authors, though, they're still a fantastic way to find new readers almost instantly.

As with most forms of book marketing, discount promo sites are not likely to revolutionise your career on their own, but they should form a large and important part of your overall strategy.

Some of the most popular promo sites are Book-Bub, Robin Reads, FreeBooksy/BargainBooksy, Fussy Librarian and Booksends.

WHEN TO APPLY FOR PROMOS

There are a few schools of thought on this, but — as with many things — my advice is to study the data and see what works best for you.

For example, if you notice a visible drop in sales at a certain point after your book has been released, it might be time to start thinking about using promos to boost sales again.

Many people quote the ethereal 'thirty day cliff', which suggests that books lose their visibility on Amazon after thirty days. I've personally never seen any evidence for this, but it might be because I've always kept up my advertising and marketing efforts — even towards my backlist — and have a steady stream of readers making their way through my series.

PROMO STACKING

Promo stacking follows the advice that you should strike while the iron's hot. By arranging discount promos with a number of websites across the same period of time, you can capitalise on the secondary effects of these sites.

As a quick aside, most vendors have a ranking algorithm which rewards strong long-term sales in some form or another. For example, Amazon's algorithm is widely accepted to count yesterday's sales 50% as important as today's, and the day before's as 50% as important as yesterday's (so 25% as important as today's). In other words, the effect halves as you move back a day.

A one-day BookBub Featured Deal, then, is unlikely to top the Amazon charts (or even come close) as it will be a one-day spike rather than sustained strong sales.

That's why many authors advocate promo stacking, in which you have promos running each day for a week or two, building those 'long term' sales (if a week can be considered long term).

Personally, although I accept the theory is sound, I consider the whole exercise to be far less valuable than many other authors.

As I mentioned earlier in the book, sales ranking is nowhere near as important as it used to be. Almost all vendors are moving away from it in terms of visibility, and others (such as Kobo) have never prioritised it as a way of displaying books in front of users.

So, although promo stacking might well get your book higher up the vendors' charts, what's the point if potential readers don't even look at those charts?

1. Decide which launch strategy you're going to go with. Overall, don't panic too much about launch day, week or even month. This is about the long-term.
2. Contact book bloggers and ensure they've got the time and availability to review your new release. This is best done as early as possible to ensure you get a slot, but don't worry about the reviews going live before or around the time of release. Some fresh PR love a few weeks later can be hugely valuable.
3. Consider the different forms of paid advertising to bring fresh eyes to your books on an ongoing basis.
4. Form a mailing list strategy. At the very least, ensure you have a mailing list and

advertise it in the back of your books —
and on your website — with a truly
enticing reason for readers to join.

5. Consider using discount promotion sites to
   funnel lots of readers into your series or
   create some buzz around your books.

STAGE 6: POST LAUNCH

AMEND YOUR OTHER BOOKS

The concept of readthrough is absolutely vital in indie publishing.

Let me explain.

If you buy one of my books at $4.99, I earn a $3.49 royalty. That's great. But it's even better if that's the first book of my series of ten.

If you then go on to buy the whole series, I'll earn a total royalty of $34.90 across the ten books. But that'll only happen if readers know about my other books.

In the back of each of mine, I have adverts for my other books. If it's a series title, I'll advertise the next book in the series. That way, readers can funnel themselves through your canon and read each of your books in turn.

If it's not a series title, but instead is a standalone

novel, I advertise my other standalones or funnel readers through into my main series.

If your new title is in an existing series, make sure you update the back matter of the *previous* title to advertise your new book. Likewise, if it's a standalone book you should promote it in the back matter of your other standalone books.

Similarly, where are you sending readers after they've finished reading *this* book, the one you're launching? Think about the funnel and the reader journey. Where do you want them to go next? Don't let your book be a satellite and simply leave readers floating adrift with nowhere else to go.

If you use Vellum (and you really should use Vellum), this is extremely easy. You can tell Vellum the sales links for each vendor, and it'll automatically put the correct vendor's link in your book file depending on whether it's creating the Kindle, Kobo or Apple file. That way, you won't fall foul of any vendors' rules. For example, Apple won't let you even *mention* Amazon in a book file, even less link to their website.

Knowing who your readers are and respecting the platform they want to read on is vital. *Don't* just funnel everyone through to Amazon or your author website and expect them to be happy. At best, that's lazy. At worst, it's downright disrespectful. Readers deserve your respect.

Do your books contain a list of the full series at

the front or back? Make sure your new book is added to each of these lists. What about your book descriptions at the vendors? Do you need to update lists there, too? Make sure everything is accurate and up to date, or you'll haemorrhage readers.

EXPLOITING THE FUNNEL

If your new book is part of a funnel — that is, part of an existing series or group of linked books — this is something on which you can capitalise.

If, for example, you've just launched book two in a series (or even book eight), it might be worth considering applying for a BookBub Featured Deal on the first book in the series.

Featured Deals can send huge amounts of traffic to your book and, therefore, to your series. It's not uncommon to see 30,000 or 40,000 downloads of a free book in one day using BookBub Featured Deals. If only 1% of those open the book, read it and want to carry on with the series, that's another 300 or 400 readers you can funnel through.

Let's do the maths.

As I write this, I've just been accepted for my latest BookBub Featured Deal. It's for *Too Close for*

Comfort, the first book in my Knight & Culverhouse police procedural series, which will be free for the period of the promotion.

This Featured Deal cost me $642.13 for a one-day worldwide promotion, and I'm told I can expect an estimated 37,800 downloads.

The 1% figure I used above is a conservative one. I'm a realist, and I know most of those 37,800 readers won't even open my book. I haven't opened the vast majority of the free books on my devices, either.

Even if 10% of them open it and read it, I'll be conservative and assume only 10% of *them* will want to carry on with the series. There's my 1% lower-end readthrough estimate.

I currently have eight books in the series, priced as follows:

Book 2: $3.99 ($2.79 royalty)
Book 3: $4.99 ($3.49 royalty)
Book 4: $4.99 ($3.49 royalty)
Book 5: $4.99 ($3.49 royalty)
Book 6: $4.99 ($3.49 royalty)
Book 7: $4.99 ($3.49 royalty)
Book 8: $4.99 ($3.49 royalty)

That's a total potential royalty of $23.73 if a reader buys the whole series.

If 1% of my BookBub downloaders (378 people)

buy the whole series, that'll net me $8,969. On a spend of $642.

Even if 1% of them go on to buy book 2 only, I'll make $1,054 on a spend of $642, almost doubling my money.

Just 1% of readers.

What if 10% of them love the series enough to buy the whole lot? We're potentially talking almost $90,000 of income from a $642 spend.

And this isn't just pie-in-the-sky thinking, by the way. In October 2018, BookBub's own data showed that almost 75% of their readers buy full-price books as well as discounted ones. The average price of those books they buy? Between $6 and $7.

The fact of the matter is that readers are more than willing to pay a decent price for books in a series they love, and funnelling people in with a free first-in-series is a brilliant way to get them hooked on your books.

THE PERMAFREE DEBATE

I get asked a lot whether I think permafree (having a book **perma**nently **free**) is still a good strategy in the modern market.

To give this some context, the early days of digital publishing were awash with authors giving away the first book in their series for free, as a method of tempting readers to try their books — and in the hope of them going on to buy more.

This was nothing new. It was the literary equivalent of the guy in the supermarket letting you try a new sausage or bit of pretzel, before letting you know where you can buy some more if you happen to like it enough. There are a lot of books out there, so why would readers want to part with good money and take a chance on an author they don't know and haven't heard of?

Permafree became less effective with the introduction of KDP Select and Kindle Unlimited, because Amazon-based readers could get books effectively for free anyway, by subscribing to KU. And the authors still got paid (just about).

That, along with the huge proliferation of free books on the platform, led to a decline in the effectiveness of permafree on Amazon. I can see exactly why, too. I must have about 150 free books on my Kindle. I estimate I've probably read six or seven of them. And I doubt I'm the worst offender.

Other vendors don't have the same problems. The KU model has not been replicated, for example, on Apple Books, Kobo, NOOK or Google Play. And there are very good reasons for that. (Kobo does have Kobo Plus in Belgium and the Netherlands, but — crucially — it does not require exclusivity.)

As a result, readthrough from free to paid is much, much higher on Apple Books, Kobo, NOOK and Google Play than it is on Amazon. As a general rule, we can be talking many multiples of Amazon's percentage readthrough rate.

Readers on those platforms are, generally speaking, more serious readers and far less likely to be freebie seekers. That means that when a free book is available, they're far more appreciative of it. Those markets aren't flooded with free. Free is — rather counterintuitively, perhaps — given far more value. As a result, readthrough is much higher.

So, if you're wide with your books (and you'll not be surprised by now to hear me insist that you should be) permafree is still an extremely viable business decision.

Kobo and Apple Books recommend permafree as a successful and suggested strategy on their platforms. And they'd know. They've got the figures right in front of them.

So, although free doesn't work anywhere near as well at Amazon as it used to, it's highly recommended as a strategy for Apple Books, Kobo, NOOK and Google Play.

If you're wide, go permafree with your first in series. If you're in Kindle Unlimited, your books are effectively free anyway, so the argument is null and void.

MORE PAID ADVERTISING

WHAT PAID ADVERTISING SHOULD I BE DOING?

Again, this is a case where one size certainly does not fit all. The answer will be different for every author. It even changes for me depending on what sort of book I'm writing.

For example, my psychological thrillers with domestic hooks rely heavily on Facebook advertising. The type of hooks those books have is ideal for grabbing people's attention while they're in a social mood or situation. They're also fantastic for finding readers who might not be keen bookworms, but are highly intrigued by the premise.

My series books, however, tend to appeal to more regular readers, and as such often do better being advertised using Amazon Advertising and BookBub Ads.

It's a case of experimenting and seeing what works best for you. Unfortunately, there is no magic bullet. Anyone offering one is likely being disingenuous at best.

IS PAID ADVERTISING NECESSARY?

This has always been a point of discussion in the industry. However, I can't think of a single successful indie author who hasn't used paid advertising to some substantial degree.

The debate, though, is now largely over.

Beginning sometime around August or September 2018, Amazon made some changes to their backend systems. They do the same around this time every year, but the 2018 changes hurt a lot of authors.

At the time of writing we're still trying to ascertain exactly what happened, but one thing we do know is that organic visibility of books has nosedived.

Coincidentally, this happened around the same time as the Amazon Advertising platform came out of the testing phase and was renamed and rebranded, with Amazon enticing authors to pay to advertise their books on Amazon — as well as giving them 30% (or 65%) of every book sold. Funny, that.

Many authors and commentators noticed that the Also Boughts were starting to disappear. These are the 'Customers who bought this item also bought' recommendations on each Amazon product page, designed to help readers find books which are similar to the one they're currently looking at.

Lo and behold, the Also Boughts were replaced by a carousel of sponsored products — all placed there by authors using Amazon Advertising. Who'd have guessed?

In short, the largest ebook retailer appears to be doing whatever it can to increase authors' reliance on their paid advertising platform and eliminating other ways in which readers can discover your books.

This is, of course, hugely short-sighted. It erodes customers' trust in Amazon, because Amazon's previously-trusted recommendation systems are no longer in control. Advertisers are. The books Amazon recommends to readers are no longer the books the reader is likely to actually want or enjoy — they're the ones the advertisers have paid the most money to have placed there.

I've no idea why Amazon, previously the doyenne of long-term thinking in the online sphere, has so flagrantly shifted its focus to such incredibly short-term, reputation-damaging thinking, but it has. And, for now, authors have to live with it.

In short, paid advertising is more important than ever before. If you disagree with Amazon's stance and methods of forcing authors to spend money through Amazon Advertising, there are plenty of other paid advertising avenues available to authors. It's not a stance I hold personally, though. Mine's more crossed arms and one raised eyebrow, as I look over the rim of my glasses at them.

WHAT, THAT'S IT?

As I've mentioned earlier in this book and in numerous other places, I don't intend to write a book — or even a section of a book — on how to market your books successfully. There are a few reasons for this.

Firstly, the industry changes exceptionally quickly. By the time I'd written the book, a huge percentage of it would then be inaccurate and out of date. Secondly, my outlook is very much a long-term one. I'm not interested in short-term gold rushes (my computer autocorrected that to 'short-term goldfishes', which I'm not interested in either).

It's also true to say that what works for me won't work for you. I don't even have a single surefire strategy for my own books. I use various different strategies for my different series and books. There is no magic bullet.

If you want to look at further avenues to explore, though, I'd recommend Facebook Ads, Amazon Advertising (for Amazon books) and BookBub Ads (for everything else).

Current trends and up-to-the-minute advice can be found in my Facebook group.

To learn how to advertise your books through these media in a LOT more detail than I could ever offer, I'd strongly recommend Mark Dawson's Ads for Authors course. There's also a pretty nifty *BookBub Ads for Authors* module presented by yours truly.

1. Change the back matter in your other books to reflect your new release and funnel readers through your books.
2. Exploit the funnel. Ensure readers can find their way through your series and move on to the next book at the exact point they want more: when they've just finished one of yours.
3. Consider paid advertising on an ongoing basis to continue to drive new readers to your books.

THE CHECKLIST

A SHORT NOTE

If something needs saying, it needs saying numerous times.

This checklist is the one I personally use when planning my next book. It works for me. It might well work for you. It'll probably need some tweaking to suit your own preferred schedule or the particular quirks of your genre.

Either way, it should provide a decent framework for you when planning your next release, and in any case will serve as an insurance policy to ensure you've taken care of everything at each stage. It's a complicated process, and things are easily forgotten.

The eagle-eyed amongst you will notice that the checklist doesn't always follow the same order as the sections in the book you've just read. That's because many of the processes (paid advertising, mailing list strategies) actually cover or encompass many different stages of the process. The nature of a book, though, means each item had to have its home somewhere. Where possible, I included it in the stage where it's most prominently used. The following checklist, though, splits them out and shows you where and how each piece of advice is used at each stage.

PLOTTING AND PLANNING

- Decide on genre and classification.
- Find the hook.
- Find your beginning (inciting incident), middle (irreversible event) and end.
- Flesh this out into a full 'this then that' synopsis.
- Identify and list the beats of your novel.
- Begin writing, using each beat as a chapter, with a clear roadmap of where you're going at all times.

DURING THE WRITING PHASE

- If you get stuck, try visualising the finished product to spur you on.
- If you need an extra piece of motivation, commission a cover.
- Likewise, write the blurb. Clearing the hook and theme of the story can get you over the finish line.
- Consider the book's title. You can't go anywhere without this.
- Plan your pre-order strategy.
- Email your mailing list with a teaser about your book.

COMING TO THE END OF WRITING

- Do some keyword research for Amazon subcategory rankings.
- Organise the formatting of your book.
- If it hasn't already been done, commission a cover and write a blurb.
- Finalise the book's title.
- Share your cover and blurb with your mailing list.
- Contact book bloggers.

BUILDING UP TO YOUR LAUNCH

The following should only be done once you've decided on your launch date and are actively working towards it, with your title already actively available for pre-order at all stores.

- Consider paid advertising for your pre-order book.
- Let your mailing list know the book's available for pre-order.
- Update the back matter of your previous books, ensuring you link to the new one.
- Add the book to your website.
- Add the book to your BookBub profile.
- Arrange a Pre-Order Alert and New Release Alert for your book at BookBub.
- Claim your book at Amazon Author Central — in all territories.
- Explore and arrange potential audiobook production.
- 'Last chance' emails to your mailing list.
- Consider using discount promotion sites to push your earlier series books and funnel new readers through to the next release.

THE LAUNCH

- Engage paid advertising.
- Email your mailing list to let them know the book's now out, and ask for reviews once they've read it.

POST LAUNCH

- Funnel new readers into the top of your series if the new release is part of one.
- Remind your mailing list to get the book and leave a review.
- Explore more paid advertising avenues if early results are good.
- If not already done, ensure the back matter of your other books directs readers towards this one.
- Start planning your next book!

RECOMMENDED READING

This is a non-exhaustive list of books and resources which will provide further information on subjects I've touched on in this book, or which I highly recommend as further reading.

PLOTTING & PLANNING

Into the Woods
John Yorke
A guide to story structure and writing books that capture imaginations.

The Marshall Plan for Novel Writing
Evan Marshall

An often-overlooked guide to planning a novel, and the one which formed the bulk of my own personal model.

13 Steps to Evil: How to Craft Superbad Villains
Sacha Black
No book is complete without its antagonist, or villain. This book shows you how to create compelling ones.

10 Steps To Hero : How To Craft A Kickass Protagonist
Sacha Black
From the writer of the above, this book outlines how writing a compelling hero can transform your book.

OVERCOMING ROADBLOCKS

59 Seconds: Think a little, change a lot
Richard Wiseman
As far as I'm concerned, Richard Wiseman is God. In this book he shows you, amongst other things, how visualisation can change your life.

PRE-LAUNCH CONSIDERATIONS

The Author's Guide to Cover Design

Stuart Bache

The definitive book for authors on how to consider cover design and work with cover designers, written by my own cover designer and good friend, Stuart Bache.

KDP Rocket

Kindlepreneur

Not a book, but a great piece of software for keyword research. You can download it from https://croft.link/KDPRocket.

Vellum

180g

Another software recommendation, this time for formatting beautiful books. I use Vellum for all my books. You can download it from http://vellum.pub.

LAUNCH AND BEYOND

Ads for Authors

Mark Dawson

This is an online course in advertising for authors. Highly recommend. This is the course that changed my way of thinking about marketing my books, and which transformed my career. https://croft.link/AdsForAuthors

Newsletter Ninja

Tammi Labrecque

A great guide to using your mailing list to help grow your career and author brand.

Help! My Facebook Ads Suck

Michael Cooper

A guide to spotting problems with your Facebook ads and knowing how to use the system to your advantage.

WANT MORE?

Thank you for reading *The Indie Author Checklist*.

If you're interested in any future books I write for authors, please click here to join my mailing list: http://indieauthormindset.com/

I'll email you when I have new books available and, as a thank-you for joining, you'll get an exclusive discount off the launch price of each book.

And please check out the official Facebook group at https://www.facebook.com/groups/IndieAuthorMindset/.

Thank you once again for reading *The Indie Author Checklist*.